The Book of Shiva

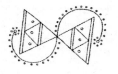

The Book of
Shiva

NAMITA GOKHALE

PENGUIN
ANANDA

PENGUIN ANANDA
Published by the Penguin Group
Penguin Books India Pvt. Ltd, 11 Community Centre, Panchsheel Park,
New Delhi 110 017, India
Penguin Group (USA) Inc., 375 Hudson Street, New York,
New York 10014, USA
Penguin Group (Canada), 90 Eglinton Avenue East, Suite 700, Toronto,
Ontario, M4P 2Y3, Canada (a division of Pearson Penguin Canada Inc.)
Penguin Books Ltd, 80 Strand, London WC2R 0RL, England
Penguin Ireland, 25 St Stephen's Green, Dublin 2, Ireland (a division of
Penguin Books Ltd)
Penguin Group (Australia), 707 Collins Street, Melbourne, Victoria 3008,
Australia (a division of Pearson Australia Group Pty Ltd)
Penguin Group (NZ), 67 Apollo Drive, Rosedale, Auckland 0632,
New Zealand (a division of Pearson New Zealand Ltd)
Penguin Group (South Africa) (Pty) Ltd, 24 Sturdee Avenue, Rosebank,
Johannesburg 2196, South Africa

Penguin Books Ltd, Registered Offices: 80 Strand, London WC2R 0RL,
England

First published in Viking by Penguin Books India 2001
Published in Penguin Books 2009
Published in Penguin Ananda 2012

Text copyright © Namita Gokhale 2001
Illustrations copyright © Penguin Books India 2001
Illustrations by Amitabh

All rights reserved

10 9 8 7 6 5 4 3 2 1

ISBN 9780143419891

Typeset in Sabon by Mantra Virtual Services, New Delhi
Printed at Repro India Ltd., Navi Mumbai

ALWAYS LEARNING   **PEARSON**

For Meru and Shivani,
both daughters of the mountains

Contents

Introduction

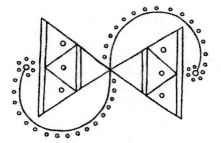

Shiva has 1008 names which describe his attributes. Chanting these guarantees his grace. The scope, diversity and contrary polarities which lie behind the meanings of these names evoke the truly unknowable nature of Shiva. Let us begin with an evocation of 108 of these names.

Achaleshvar: immovable lord, the resolute one; Adi-Nath: primeval master; Aghora: non-terrifying, pleasing; Aja: unmanifest; Aja-Ekapada: one-footed lord; Ajagandhi: he who smells like a goat; Akrura: kind god; Andhakehsvar: dispeller of darkness; Antak: the ender; Apamnidhi: lord of the waters (semen); Ardhanari: half woman; Ashani: thunderbolt; Asutosh: easily pleased; Avadhut: naked ascetic; Baleshvar: long-haired; strong; Basava: bull; Bhairava: quick-tempered god; Bhasmeshvar: smeared with ash; Bhava: existence; Bhikshatan: celestial beggar; Bhima: strong one; Bhisma: terrible one; Bhola: simpleton, guileless god; Bhootpati: god of ghosts; Bhuteshvara: lord of elements; Bhuvanesh: lord of the world; Bilva-Dandin: bearer of a staff of belva; Chandrachuda: moon-crested; Dakshineshvar: god who faces the south; Damarudharin: bearer of the rattle-drum; Ekavratya: unorthodox sage; Gajantaka: killer of the elephant demon; Gambhiresh: austere ascetic; Ganapati: lord of ganas; Gangadhar: bearer of the river Ganga; Ghora: fearsome; Girisha: lord of the hills; **Grihapati:** householder; **Guheshvar:** lord of the caves, mysterious one; **Hara:** router, seizer, ravisher; **Hiranyaretas:** lord of the golden seed; **Ishana:** lord; **Ishvara:** godhead; **Jambukeshvar:** lord of Jambudvipa i.e. India; **Jateshvar:** lord with matted hair; **Jimutavahan:** he who rides the clouds; **Jvareshvar:** lord of fevers; **Kaleshvar:** lord of time, lord of art; **Kamandaludhari:** bearer of the water-pot; **Kamanashe:** destroyer of desire; **Kapalin:** bearer of skulls; **Kapardin:** lord with a conch-shaped topknot; **Karpure-Gauranga:** white as camphor; **Kedar:** lord of the hills; **Kiraata:** tribal; **Krittivasa:** he who wears animal hide; **Lakulisha:** bearer of the staff; **Mahabaleshvar:** almighty one; **Mahadeva:** great god; **Maharshi:** great sage; **Mahesh:** great lord; **Maithuneshvar:** lord of sexual union; **Manish:** conqueror of the mind; **Marutta:** wind, storm; **Nageshvar:** lord of serpents; **Nagnavratadhari:** naked sage; **Nataraja:** lord of dance and drama; **Neelkantha:** blue-necked one; **Omkarnath:** lord of the mystical syllable 'Om'; **Pashaye:** lord of the noose; **Pashupati:** lord of the beasts; **Pavaka:** fire, lava; **Purusha:** cosmic spirit, the primeval man; **Rudra:** wild god, howler; **Sadjoyta:** eternally radiant; **Sailesh:** lord of mountains; **Samhari:** destroyer; **Sarva:** archer; **Shambhu:** benign; **Shanker:** benevolent, beneficent; **Sharabha:** dragon; **Shikhandin:** lord with a peacock plume; **Siddhartha:** one who is accomplished; **Somasundara:** beautiful as the moon; **Somnath:** lord of soma, the herb of vitality; **Sthanu:** the great pillar, that which is still; **Sundarmurti:** alluring body; **Svashva:** master of dogs; **Tamasopati:** lord of inertia, darkness, passivity; **Tejomaya:** radiant being; **Trilochan:** three-eyed; **Tripurantaka:** destroyer of the demon cities; **Trishuldhari:** bearer of the trident; **Ugra:** fierce; **Umapati:** husband of Uma-Parvati; **Urdhvalinga:** aroused linga (life-force); **Vaidyanath:** lord of physicians; **Vamadev:** lord of the left-handed (tantric) paths; **Vibhuti-Bhushan:** he who is bedecked with ash marks; **Vinapani:** he who plays the lute; **Virabhadra:** the noble hero; **Vireshvar:** lord of martial arts; **Virupaksha:** lord with ill-formed malignant eyes; **Vishvanath:** lord of the universe; **Vrikshanath:** lord of trees; **Vrishabhanath:** tamer of bulls; **Yakshanath:** lord of yakshas, forest-spirits; **Yogesh:** lord of yoga

Let us meditate on Lord Shiva, the supreme ascetic. He wears the crescent moon on his forehead, from which flows the celestial river Ganga. The river represents the ceaseless flux of time and is the embodiment of the nurturing life-force. Shiva's body is smeared with ash, and a tiger skin is girt around his loins. Of his four arms, one carries a trident, one an axe, and the other two are set in classical mudras, granting boons and removing fear.

Lord Shiva has three eyes, through which he can

view the past, the present and the future. The third eye, that of higher perception, looks inwards. When its vision is directed outwards, the searing intensity of its gaze emblazons and destroys all it looks at. The three-eyed aspect of Shiva is variously referred to as Virupaksha, Triaksha, Trinayana and Trinetra.

The crescent moon rests like a diadem on Shiva's long matted hair. According to myth, Soma, the moon, was discredited by an assembly of the gods for some indiscretion and so cast into the ocean. Later, during the *samudra manthan*, the churning of the ocean, Shiva resurrected Soma by placing the moon on his brow, thereby restoring the intuitive faculties to their rightful position.

The trident of Shiva, his trishul, represents the triad of the creator, the preserver and the destroyer. His spear, the pashupata, is the weapon with which he destroys the universe at the dissolution of the yugas, the ordained time cycles. His axe is called the parashu, which he gifted to Parashurama. He also carries a club called the khatvanga, which has a skull at its head. Around his neck is a garland of skulls, which earns him the epithet of Kapalin. The drum in his hand, the damaru, heralds the dance of creation, just as the ashes which anoint him signify the forces of destruction ever present in all that is living.

Shiva is accompanied in popular iconography by

his wife Parvati, a beauteous ever-auspicious figure who shares his austerities and penance. Seated beside them is their son Ganesha, the elephant-headed remover of obstacles, and Skanda, or Kartika, their second son. The sacred bull Nandi, representing the powers of fecundity, procreation and constancy, is also a member of this divine family.

Shiva is the god of life and death, of destruction and rebirth. The whole life process is imminent in him, but he transcends it and inhabits a mental, emotional and spiritual space which is difficult to understand through intellectual processes alone. To embrace Shiva, to comprehend his power, involves an intuitive leap into our deepest inner selves.

I am writing this book as an act of devotion, not presumption. The mythopoeic mind assigns attributes to godheads, visible symbols to unrepresentable mysteries. The attributes of a saguna, qualified god, is therefore completely different from the non-attributes of a nirguna, non-qualified god. Hindu divinity gives us an infinite variety and hierarchy of gods and goddesses to worship and aspire to, so that we may seek the version of saguna reality most suited to the accidental permutations of our personality and situation.

The Puranic tales recounted in this book contain a sense of timelessness. They are elastic and energetic and in a constant state of reinterpretation and reinvention.

There has always been a remarkable flexibility between the oral and written traditions, and the immensely popular television mega-serials on the Hindu gods are an appropriation of technology and media by an ancient and uninterrupted culture. The *Ramayana* and *Mahabharata* television epics, aired on the national channel Doordarshan in the late 1980s and early 1990s created the conditions for the revival of both moderate and fundamental religious forces in India. While the Epic of Gilgamesh, the Odyssey, the Illiad and even the Old Testament may lose their immediate relevance to society, the Hindu sacred and religious literature reinsinuates itself back into the mainstream of life and technology with a startling contemporaneity.

India, with its infamous lack of the historical sense of time, with its non-linear approach to ideas and events, has managed to retain a sense of the dynamic and the interactive with reference to its mythology. The gods are still alive in India. They are not symbols or emblems of abstract conceptions, but vibrant anthropomorphic realities in the living faith of the river of Hinduism, flowing uninterrupted from the beginning of historically recorded time.

Lord Shiva is one aspect of the holy trinity of Brahma, Vishnu and Mahesh. Brahma is the creator and preceptor of life. Vishnu is the preserver of the divine movement of life, representing the forces of balance and equilibrium. Mahesh, another name of Shiva, is the greatest of the gods, for he alone is the god of death and resurrection, of the flux of being and non-being.

Shiva is the primeval, primordial aspect of these enduring and eternal forces. His worship is not for the weak minded, for the vision of the universe that Shiva offers us is as stark as it is magnificent. Shiva's father-in-law, Himavata, is the lord of riches and wealth, but the supreme ascetic disdains mere wealth and demands of his followers a life of awesome austerity and penances. Kubera, the god of wealth, owes allegiance to none other than the Lord Shiva, yet Shiva himself is a naked ascetic with a skull for a begging bowl.

The evolution of Shiva as both a concept and an anthropomorphic figure is a movement as natural as the flow of the river of faith. Shiva first appears in the historical consciousness in the figure of Pashupati, on the seals of Mohenjodaro, 2500 BC. This early iconography portrays Shiva seated in a yogic posture, in the Siddhasana, with feet crossed beneath the erect penis, the urdhva linga. The image bears three faces and with two arms. He is surrounded in this seal by representations of an elephant, a tiger, a rhinoceros and a buffalo. Similar seals of a deity holding a trident and accompanied by a bull have also been found at these sites. Over the millennia the iconic image changes, but never essentially. The accretations of myth and interpretation cannot shake this austere and enduring ascetic.

There have been suggestions of a degree of lateral influence by the Dionysic cults on the ecstatic ritual aspects of Shiva worship in the Indian subcontinent. The Greeks who came to India around 300 BC found commonalties with their own god Zagreus-Dionysius. The Indo-Aryan god did share some attributes in common, as in the convergence of the Varuna-Uranus myths. Dionysus was, like Shiva, a priapic god, characteristically symbolized by an erect phallus. The vine leaf was sacred to him, as the leaf of the belva was sacred to Lord Shiva. Shiva's ganas corresponded with the satyrs of the Orphic mystery cults. Like Shiva, Dionysus had a temperament which could concede of excess, and like Shiva, he was associated with hills and mountains. Greek myth and literature both record the Indian sojourns of these gods, and among others, Megasthanes has written about the travels to India of essentially Greek gods such as Dionysus, god of the hills, and Hercules, god of the plains. Some scholars, however, suggests that the identification was perhaps a form of convenient cultural annexation during the course of Alexander's Indian campaign.

The identities of the celestials and the demons have of course changed constantly with the terrain, with geographical as well as historical compulsions. The

divine ahuras of Persia and Asia Minor became the
asuras of Hindu demonology, just as the devatas of the
Indian subcontinent transmuted by reversal into
daemonic beings. There is much that is common in the
mythological structures of the Proto-Aryans and from
the time of the composition of the Avesta, there is a
complete polarity of interpretations regarding the
character of Vedic and Avestan mythic figures. Those
beings who are gods in India metamorphose into demons
(daevas) in the Avesta, and the ahuras (gods) become
the asuras of the Indian subcontinent. The Vedic
pantheon distinguished between the gods and demons
in that the former were blessed by the celestial rta, or
law and righteousness, while the demons yielded to
maya, or the power of illusion and delusion.

Many indigenous tribal myths have also converged
and been appropriated into the mainstream of the Shiva
cult. The cult of Rudra-Shiva shows distinct influences
of the great Shamanic tradition of Siberia and Central
Asia. This ancient Shamanistic ethos had devolved into
the pre-Buddhist traditions of the ancient religion of the
Bon-po, and was also concurrent with the local
Shamanistic religious systems of the aboriginal tribes of
India. The use of the skull and the skeleton in mystical
ceremony and much of the Tantric approach shares
common antecedents with these traditions, as
demonstrated in Mircea Eliade's seminal work on the

spread of Shamanism.

Yet the philosophical unity in the concept of Shiva is not breached or violated by these contrary and often contradictory visions. The dreaming god of the mountains continues to hold the entirety of the created and uncreated world in the inner vision of his third eye.

The Manifestations of Shiva

Shiva's manifestations are complex and contradictory, for he is the all-encompassing reality who resolves all polarities in his being. His auspicious and terrible aspects are all mirrors of the same primary self.

Shiva is the god who must not be named, for to name is to limit and curtail; yet his many names together constitute the sum of his unknowable mysteries. The many realities of the multifaceted Shiva are encompassed by the aspects described in his different manifestations. These constitute a poetic, mythic rendering of the world-reality, a sakshat or saguna naming of the unnamable, inscrutable mysteries of the nirguna or unqualified godhead.

Rudra: In the Vedas, Shiva appears as Rudra, the howler. He is the embodiment of the 'Great Fear', of the thunderbolt. Harbinger of both rain and prosperity, he is entirely fearful in his terrible beauty. Raudra or Rudra is he whose name is not uttered, the Wild God of the Rig Veda, the First One, the god who is invoked by what one commentator refers to as a 'lucid frenzy'. As Rudra came into being, he brought the mysteries of creation and the manifest with him. When he approached, he howled, (arodit), and so came to be known as Rudra, the roarer. In his manifestation as the lord of the thunderbolts, he encompasses Agni, the element of fire. Like Agni, he both sustains and destroys life. In the primordial and timeless moment of creation, Agni brought forth the seed of heaven, through Prajapati, the first Father.

As Rudra, is associated then, as now, with Agni, so is he associated with Bhairava, the destructive aspect of Rudra. He is also the embodiment of the sun, the element of cosmic fire, and in this form his son is the planet Saturn, born of his wife Survarchala. As Rudra is among the solar divinities, he is invoked as Bhuteshvara, the lord of elements. Later the bhutas came to be perceived as ghosts and spirits, and consequently Bhuteshvara became the god of spirits and ghosts. In his aspect as Bhuteshvara, Rudra-Shiva frequents the cremation grounds, where, besmeared by the bhasma, a word connoting both destruction and ashes, he contemplates the continuity of death and life, of being and non-being. He wears a garland of skulls and, encircled by serpents, another potent symbol of cosmic continuity, he holds ascendancy over the hierarchy of imps, goblins and demons that thrive in the dark aspect of consciousness.

The polarity of Rudra-Shiva, of the destructive and benevolent realities of the godhead, became embodied in the Ashtamurti, the eight aspects of Shiva. Of these eight names, Rudra, Sarva, Ugra or Ashani and Bhima refer to his destructive aspect, and Bhava, Pashupati, Mahadeva and Ishana to the benevolent aspect. None of these versions is complete in itself, for only when they conjoin do the magnificent forces of creation and destruction become manifest.

Sarva: After Rudra, the next aspect of Shiva is Sarva, the Archer. Sarva represents the element earth, or Prithvi. As the son of Earth, Bhumi, he is called Bhauma, the earth god. His consort and feminine energy is Dharani, she who sustains. Their son is Mangala, the planet Mars. The word Sarva is derived from 'saru', meaning arrow. This arrow has three parts and is joined with Kalagni, the fire of destruction. The dispassionate mercilessness, the cruelty almost, of this manifestation of Shiva is difficult to understand for those brought up and trained in the simple polarities of good and evil. The arrow is a metaphor of Shiva's power, a parallel to the shaft of lightning which is the visible symbol of Rudra's wrath. These are the symbols natural within a hunter-gatherer and agricultural economy, but the metaphysical validity of their perception is an eternal and enduring one.

According to Hindu myth, at the inception of creation, Prajapati, the manifestation of Brahma the creator, violated his own daughter personified in the constellation Rohini (also identified with the constellation Aldebaran). This is understood philosophically as the violation of the ultimate and absolute reality, or the devolution of the unmanifest into the manifest. The great god Shiva, himself the ultimate and inviolable reality, through his manifestation as Sarva the Archer, aimed his divine arrow at Brahma-Prajapati, the father of the universe, and decapitated him, for the absolution of which he had to later suffer much penance.

The syllable Om is the bow, the Atman (self) is the arrow, Brahman (the ultimate reality) is the target. Carefully should it be pierced; thus one becomes united with it; with the arrow, with its target.

There is also a fascinating association of Sarva-Rudra-Shiva, of the Wild Archer, with Sirius, the Dog Star, the hound of heaven. When the sun of the vernal equinox arose in the constellation Rohini, he was the star Mrgavyadha, the archer who is the hunter of the antelope, the arrows his rays.

Whatever destroys any existing thing, moveable or stationary, at any time, is Sarva-Rudra. Sarva, as a name and form of Rudra, is invoked together with Yama, the god of death, and with Mrityu, death itself. And yet, in the spirit of contradiction and reconciliation that epitomizes Hindu metaphysics, he is also invoked in the form of Bhava, existence. The divine archer holds the power of life and death, and these are not contrary but integrated aspects of his reality. He can avert or restrain his arrows, and through this grace he can liberate from death.

Ugra: The other malefic aspects of Rudra-Shiva include

Ugra, the fearful, also called Ashani, the thunderbolt, the spark that conflagrates the fire of eternal destruction. His wife or consort-energy is Diksha, and their son is Santana or libation. In this aspect Ugra-Bhima-Ashani is the devourer of devotions, and the granter of all desires. Bhima represents the element of ether, and his consort Disha is the embodiment of the directions of space. Their son, Sarga, is representative of creation.

Pashupati: Shiva in his benign form appears as Pashupati, the herdsman, as well as Bhava, Mahadeva and Ishana. The Bhava aspect of Rudra-Shiva, the manifestation as existence, is associated with the element of water. Bhava is also recognized as Parjanya, the lord of rain. His consort is Uma and their son is the planet Shukra, or Venus.

As Pashupati, the deity is the embodiment of the fire element. In this aspect, he is the feeder of sacrifices, and his consort and feminine energy is Svaha, the goddess of invocation and propitiation during the fire ritual. Their son is Skanda, the god of war. Literally translated, Pashupati is the lord of the animals, a figure of protection in a pastoral economy. All beings in the manifest world, from the first being, the creator himself, to all others in the hierarchy of life, were his to be slain or protected. Shiva is the great liberator who unties the snares (pasha) of each pashu, of each individual life.

In the course of time he transmutes into Vastospati, the keeper of the Vaastu mysteries. Due to his association with the fire sacrifice, Rudra-Pashupati is called Vastvaya, a remainder of the sacrifice (vaastu) which remains even after the oblations have been made. This is not as arcane as it sounds, for it represents the material residue of the spiritual sacrifice.

Ishana: As Ishana, the deity is the embodiment of the element of air, and as such the nourisher of life. As Mahadeva, the great god, Shiva is represented as a priapic figure, the god with the lingam, the phallus, as his emblem. The lingam is the reproductive power that ensures the continuity of life. Shiva's semen is preserved in the chalice of the moon, and the life-force that sustains the cycle of creation is contained in him. In this aspect, his consort is Rohini, and their son the planet Mercury.

Shiva as Mahakala

Shiva as Mahakala is portrayed as Bhairava, the terrifying aspect of Rudra-Shiva. In mythology, Bhairava is so fierce that even Kala, who is the very representation of time and death, became fearful of him. So he became Kala-Bhairava, who is also Kala-Purusha, the controller of time, and Kala-Raja, its ruler, to whom time itself is subject.

Another important aspect of Shiva-Rudra is Mrityunjaya, who personifies the victory over untimely death. Pashupati, the lord of the animals, and Mrityunjaya, the liberator from death are benevolent aspects of Shiva in the Kala-Mahakala axis. Rudra was the bearer of the seed for Prajapati, the great father, and as the catalyst between the forces of the formless and the manifest, he is paradoxically both the ally and the opponent of time. Time is personified in Hindu religion and culture as Kala. According to legend, Rudra met Kala, the god of time, and in him recognized his own self, although time had only four faces and lacked the fifth face of Shiva, that which is beyond time, as personified in his transcendent aspect of Ishana.

Shiva is thus simultaneously both the personification of time as Kala, and beyond the limitations of time as Mahakala. As the Divine Archer, as Sarva, he represents linear time. The span of life (ayus) is the lived dimension of time, the duration of which the Divine Archer dictates.

Another name for the god of time, for Kala, is

Antaka, the ender, who bends the span of given linear time to the unending cycle of life and death. Yet as Rudra he is the vital breath and energy, the prana that is the inspiration of life. The lived life is constituted of the rhythmic movement of prana, of the life breath, which is the manifest life-force. The mysteries of day and night, the cycle of the seasons, are all elaborations of this dance of time and life.

Spatial time was represented by Prajapati, and the myth of Prajapati and his celestial trials is worth recording and examining. Prajapati, the antelope, was pierced by Rudra's arrow. The wounded antelope fled to the sky and became Mrgasirsa, also identified as Orion. The metaphysical explanation is that Prajapati was pierced by Rudra's arrow and so abandoned his body, for 'the body is a mere dwelling place'. Prajapati's sacrifice led to his identification with the annual cycle, with the solar year. He was renewed each spring, at the vernal equinox, when Orion rose to herald the rising sun. Then, with the passage of time, the sun moved away and rose in another star, Aldebaran. This alteration in the sky-map, this celestial change of guard of the equinoxes, was translated in the mythic imagination into the image of Prajapati moving towards Rohini, as the father of the universe was driven by desire to violate his own daughter.

Astronomical time, the vegetative cycle, is all part

of the temporal and transcendent cycle of life. Shiva is thus described as the maker of time, Kalakara, and 'he unto whom the beginning and end of the universe is gathered'. He is both of and beyond time, the point where the motionless time of eternity enters the arena of creation.

The distinction between Kala and Mahakala, between manifest and transcendent time, is a philosophical concept of great depth and magnitude. Time in creation is rhythmic, and this is why Shiva is understood as the cosmic dancer.

Another aspect of the Kala-Mahakala imagery is the concept of Sthanu, the great pillar, wherein, personified as Shiva the great yogi, time stands still, in deference to his meditations. The seeming paradox of alternating activity and withdrawal, of systole and diastole, of inward and outward breath, encompasses the dual nature of Kala and Mahakala. The mythopoeic mind uses allegory and symbol to describe conceptual and quantum reality. In the course of cosmic history, at the time of the churning of the oceans, the *samudra manthan*, Shiva swallowed the poison which had been thrown up by Vasuki, the king of the serpents of the nether world. The serpent is of course another analogue for both time and eternity, and Vasuki is another form of Ananta Nag, the cosmic serpent representative of eternal time, from whom the Kalakuta, the poison of tyrannical temporal time, rose forth.

All these images, of the great archer, the cosmic dancer, the eternal serpent, accord Shiva a place in the highest possible metaphysical levels. They represent the collective dreaming of an intelligent and evolved society that could instinctively grasp and understand great and eternally valid truths in a symbolic or poetic form.

Tandava, the Great Dance of Shiva

The arrow of Sarva, the great archer, is also called Kalagni, and represents the consuming fire of time. At the time of destruction, at the dissolution of the cosmic cycle, Kalagni-Rudra embraces the worlds in a dance of death and destruction. This is the dance of the Tandava, the death-dance of Shiva, whose primordial rhythm heralds the beginning and end of all life.

As Shiva, he of a thousand eyes, burns the whole universe in the dreadful drum-beat of his terrifying dance, the ecstasy of the unborn, unmanifest and transcendent blurs the distinctions of Kala and Mahakala into a divine unity. As the universe burns, the element of earth dissolves into water. Fire devours the water, water is dissolved into wind, wind gives way to space, the multitudes of gods dissolve into the unity of Brahman. Then the great lord separates Prakriti, which is manifest nature and substance, from Purusha or spirit. As Kalakala, the destroyer of time, Shiva is consumed by the bliss of non-being. Encircled by flames, he restitutes the divine order of the universe.

At the end of each yuga, each aeon, the great god, in his aspect as Nataraja, dances the death-dance to herald pralaya, the dissolution of the cosmos. Shiva's dance, in the words of the art historian Coomaraswamy, is 'the clearest image of the activity of God which any religion can boast of'. Fritjof Capra, in his famous book, *The Tao of Physics*, examines Shiva's Tandava in the context of a contemporary understanding. According to him, the dynamic view of the universe, as envisioned by mystics, is similar to that of modern physics. As physics has shown that the essential quality of matter is movement and rhythm and all matter is involved in a cosmic dance, so do we encounter the image of dance in Hindu mythology as a symbol of nature. This energy dance is, in Fritjof Capra's words, 'a pulsating process of creation and destruction', where not only matter but also the void participates in the cosmic dance, creating and destroying energy patterns without end. It is, incontrovertibly, as Coomaraswamy has said, 'poetry, but nonetheless science'.

Shiva–Shakti:
The Reconciliation of
Male–Female Polarities

'Shiva is but a corpse, a *shava*. Who or what, then, is this enlivening vowel sound *I*, if not the goddess Shakti, the supreme representative of movement and life . . .?'

Heinrich Zimmer

This observation finds its source in a story of Shiva and Parvati, where the goddess, in her incarnation as Kali, set about on a course of unmitigated destruction. To restrain her, Shiva turned into a corpse and blocked her path. The goddess regretted her death-play and with the power of her shakti or feminine energy, revived Shiva, transforming him from a shava or an inert corpse into Shiva, the master of the universe.

Shiva is an anthropomorphic god, but his representation is not only in the masculine aspect. As Ardhnarishwara, half man and half woman, he encompasses and transcends the male–female contrarieties, much as he straddles the Kala-Mahakala paradox in his Kala-Bhairava form. The goddess is Shiva's shakti or power, she is his feminine energy, his consort, both cause and manifestation of his maya, of his divine play.

The concept of Sadashiva, or eternal Shiva, encompasses the state in which Shiva and Shakti are united. Sadashiva's left side is female and right side male; the two polarities are amalgamated through the mystic arousal of the Kundalini, the spinal serpent force through which the human consciousness rises in the process of its spiritual evolution.

Indian myth can be overwhelming in its complexity, but the androgynous figure of Shiva–Shakti strikes a universal chord in its profound understanding of both sexuality and the nature of the male–female configuration. The Shiva–Shakti myths illustrate a higher understanding of both gender and sexuality. Legend holds that, on the request of Brahma and Vishnu, the other members of the holy trinity, Shiva agreed to marry Sati, the daughter of the great sage Daksha. Daksha was the son of Aditi, the mother of the gods. The marriage of Shiva and Sati was solemnized in the presence of the gods and the sages, after which they went to Mount Mandara, Shiva's abode in Mount Kailash, where the supreme ascetic resumed his awesome austerities.

Sati was the first of the sixty daughters of Daksha. She was an incarnation of the eternal goddess who had taken human shape to assume her destiny as Shiva's shakti. Twenty-seven of her sisters were given in marriage to the Moon, and they became the Nakshatras, the twenty-seven lunar mansions. Sati herself was the essential primordial goddess, Kalika, the dark one, Chandika, the fierce, and Durga, the impregnable. In her self-born manifestation as Daksha's daughter, Sati was also known as Uma, which some commentators link to the Sumerian mother goddess Unu, and with Ummo, the name of the goddess who is Shiva's consort as inscribed in some Kushan coins of the reign of the King Huviska. It also refers to her extreme asceticism; to the exclamation of 'U Ma!' (no more!) uttered in response to her penances.

Sati's father, Daksha, was a great ritualistic. He organized a magnificent yagna, a sacrifice to the gods, at the holy confluence of the river Ganga at Prayag, which is modern day Allahabad. All the divinities were invited to this yagna, to the exclusion of Lord Shiva, who was deliberately insulted and treated like an outcaste by the other gods. Daksha cursed Shiva to lose his share of the sacrifice, and so no shares of the ritual oblations were offered to Rudra-Shiva. Shiva could not, of course, be cursed, for he was himself the embodiment of both the sacrifice and the sacrificial rite. After the monsoons Daksha held another splendid sacrifice at Ganga Dvara in the foothills of the Himalayas. His divine son-in-law, Rudra-Shiva who he had cursed at the sacrifice at Prayag, was again pointedly not invited. The proud patriarch Daksha scorned Rudra-Shiva, who was after all, a mere Kapalin, with a skull for a begging bowl. Shiva's body was besmeared with ash from the cremation grounds, his hair was matted, he wore a garland of skulls and was constantly intoxicated by divine ecstasy. Daksha did not deem him worthy of his grand sacrifice.

Though Sati was the great goddess Kalika reborn in human form, she was not immune to human sensitivity and vulnerability. When she found the Moon, accompanied by her sister Rohini, going to the ceremonies at Ganga Dvara, she begged her husband Shiva to go and demand his rightful place at the sacrifice. Shiva refused to go, but she won his permission to attend the sacrificial ceremony. At Ganga Dvara, the site of the ritual, no portion of the ritual offerings had been put aside for Rudra-Shiva. She demanded an explanation of her father, and his scornful reply so angered her that she cast off her body as Sati, the human daughter of Daksha, to resume her formless incarnation as the eternal goddess and the mother of the universe.

When Shiva heard of Sati's death, his rage could not be contained. He destroyed the sacrifice and cursed Daksha. Then, at the spot where Sati had immolated and consumed herself, he first took her body and smeared himself with its ashes. His hot tears burnt the earth, and even the planet Saturn, incarnate as Shanischar, was unable to contain them. Taking Sati's lifeless body in his arms, Shiva began to dance in a frenzy of love, death and despair. The gods watched in alarm as Shiva's divine frenzy began to disturb the preordained equilibrium of the universe. In an attempt to restore some order to this chaos, Vishnu's disc, his sudarshan chakra, began amputating Sati's charred body and bringing it to rest on earth. The earth became consecrated wherever a part of her body fell. Even today, the one hundred and eight Shakti pithas of Sati continue to commemorate the return to earth of the body of the eternal goddess.

After her death, the goddess was once again reborn as Parvati. She reassumed human form so that she could recombine with the masculine energies of Shiva, and so maintain the balance of Shiva–Shakti, according to the true nature of Ardhnarishwara. Parvati was the daughter of Parvata, the Mountain, and of Mena, the Woman. Parvati was born at midnight, when the constellation Mrgasiras was in conjunction with the moon. Her birth had been brought about by Kalaratri, the goddess of night, who had entered Mena's womb to become incarnate as Parvati. All this was part of an elaborate strategy by the gods to assuage Shiva's grief and persuade him to conceive a son, who, it had been prophesied, would be the destroyer of the invincible demon Taraka.

It is no coincidence that Sati, also, had a mother called Asikni, the night. The night embodied the mysteries of the great goddess, of the matriarchal religion which exalted the power of woman as the creator of life. The mountain too was an important part of the early cosmogony. Parvata and Mena had two other

daughters besides Parvati. One was Ragini, the red one,
and the other, Kutila, the curvaceous one. Parvati, as
daughter of the night, was also known as Kali, the dark
one. Kutila came to be identified with the celestial river
Ganga, and Ragini with the interstices of Dawn and
Twilight.

Parvati was born with the preordained destiny of
becoming the wife of the Great Yogi, the ascetic of
ascetics, Shiva himself. The sage Narada had read her
palm and predicted that she would marry a naked yogi
free from desire and worldly attachments, a self-born
god without mother or father. To this end, Kama, the
god of love, conspired with Rati, the goddess of lust,
and with the zephyr of spring, Vasanta, and tried to
break the course of Shiva's meditation, to direct his mind
and body towards procreation and the preservation of
the universe.

It is important to understand the role of Kama in
the scheme of Hindu mythology. Kama is the seed of
desire, which actuates the unmanifest to become
manifest. In conjunction with the feminine energies, he
ensures that the universe does not give way to stasis
and inertia, but continues to encode and replicate itself.

There is a well-known account of Shiva's first
encounter with Parvati. The great ascetic was deep in
austerities when Parvata, accompanied by his beauteous
and accomplished daughter Parvati, arrived with

offerings of flowers and fruits. Shiva was intensely attracted by Parvati, who, as Shakti, was after all only an aspect of himself, and his intense meditations were consequently disturbed. Parvati's father requested to be allowed to come daily to serve the great lord. Shiva opened his eyes and wrathfully instructed him to come without his daughter, for a woman was not needed in the company of an ascetic.

Parvati's response illustrates the philosophical and mystical basis upon which the male and female energies maintain their theological balance in Hindu culture. 'Great Shiva,' she said, 'the energy you use in the practice of your austerities is sustained by the strength of Prakriti, which is the primal cause of all action. The great lord of the linga cannot exist in isolation without his counterpart Prakriti.' Although secretly delighted by Parvati's wisdom, Shiva replied sternly that he controlled and destroyed Prakriti by his austerities, and that in his essential and ultimate reality he was without Prakriti. Parvati's reply took the issue head on: 'If you are indeed greater than Prakriti, Great Lord, then why do you practice austerities in the mountain? For everything around you is held together only by Prakriti; what you see, hear, eat, all that you are, and all that is around you, is only a manifestation of Prakriti. I too am Prakriti, and you are Purusha. If you are really distinct from and superior to me, you would not fear my proximity!'

This is in essence a rejoinder to the patriarchal
seclusion of woman deities that most religious systems
underwent at some stage in their social, economic and
cultural development. Parvati's reply addresses the
Sankhya viewpoint, while Shiva's is indicative of
monistic Vedanta philosophy. The totality of Shiva's
true nature is however so all-encompassing that the
male–female Purusha–Prakriti polarities are resolved
within his androgynous Ardhanarishwara manifestation.
Parvati won Shiva through her unswerving austerities
and penances, and he married her to beget a son, and so
ensured the safety and welfare of the gods against the
invincible demon Taraka.

The marriage of Shiva–Shakti is a consummation
of all that is sacred and holy, of all that is auspicious in
the universe. At the time of his marriage to Parvati, Shiva
had to declare his lineage, as is the custom in Hindu
ceremony. The self-born one fell silent, and the sage
Narada, who was conducting the marriage, began to
play on the his five-stringed lute, the veena. Parvata,
Shiva's father-in-law, asked Narada to stop playing on
the instrument and to proceed with the ritual. The sage
Narada explained that even the gods themselves could
not tell of Shiva's parentage, for he was the essential
unmanifest reality, assuming form, shape and attributes
only at his own will and pleasure. Nada, the primordial

sound, can be taken as the origin of the manifest Shiva, and so it was that Narada chose to play the veena to announce the great yogi's lineage.

The Divine Family of Shiva

The divine family of Shiva is an integral part of Hindu consciousness. Sati and Parvati represent his feminine Shakti or active powers, while Ganesha, his genetically engineered son who incorporates an elephant's trunk with a human body, is the omnipotent and omnipresent god of knowledge and new beginnings. Shiva's other son, Kartik, is also not born from the womb, his birth being associated with a mythic form of artificial insemination.

There is a fascinating background to these myths. The gods, troubled by the evil asura Taraka, were desperately awaiting the birth of Shiva's son, for it was he who was destined to kill the demon. However, Shiva was too deep in his meditations to engage in the necessary sexual activity with his consort, the goddess Parvati. Unable to awake him from his meditation, they decided that Agni, the god of fire, should arouse Shiva. Agni was afraid of Shiva's anger, for he well remembered the fate of Kamadeva, the god of lust, who had already earned Shiva's ire and been cursed as a consequence. He overcame his misgivings, and, following the instruction of the gods and sages, concentrated on enflaming the sexuality of the divine ascetic. Shiva felt the effect of Agni's agitations, and, leaving Parvati's side asked the deities why they were provoking him. The assembled gods explained their need for Shiva's progeny, upon which the ever-beneficent Shiva agreed to part with

his semen for this purpose. As the Lord Shiva let his
seed fall to earth, Agni transmuted into a dove and
swallowed the sacred semen.

When Parvati found out what had happened she
was much angered. The life-giving force which should
have been nourished in her womb had been appropriated
by Agni on behalf of the gods, leaving her barren.
Parvati's rage knew no bounds, and she cursed the gods
to suffer the consequences of their selfish action. By the
power of her divine tongue she caused the wives and
consorts of the devatas, the divine heaven dwellers, to
remain forever barren. In retaliation to this extreme and
incensed curse, Prithvi, the Earth, cursed Parvati,
prophesying that she would never carry a child of Shiva
in her womb. It is resultant to this malediction that both
the sons of Shiva and Parvati, Skanda and Ganesha,
were not womb born. The gods too suffered for their
actions, for Parvati's words dictated that they could no
longer propagate themselves. They became static;
banished to earth, they were now worshipped only as
stone images.

The devatas, who ritually partake of anything
offered to Agni, became impregnated with Shiva's seed.
They could not endure the heat of his divine semen and
approached Lord Shiva in desperation. He told them to
vomit the semen out, which they did, and so it was once
again returned to Agni. The god of fire sought a worthy

womb for this sacred seed and deposited it into the bodies of six chaste ladies, among the wives of the seven celestial sages, the Saptrishi, who were bathing in the icy cold waters of the Ganga in the month of Magh. Only Arundhati, the wife of sage Vashishta, refrained from the temptation of warming herself before the fire of the Agni; all the others became pregnant by this artificial and improbable means. Once they realized their condition, they hastily cast off Shiva's semen, which had already assumed the form of a foetus, on top of the Himavata mountain. The six discarded wives of the sages, the Krittikas, then nursed the child they had so strangely birthed. Thus Shiva's son also came to be known as Kartik. As his six mothers nursed him simultaneously, he developed six heads in response to feed with. There are various other versions to this story, but at an allegorical level the implications clearly point towards a celestial genealogy to Shiva's offspring. The seven sages, the Saptrishi, are identified with the constellation Ursa Major and the Great Bear, and the seven Krittikas are none other than the Pleides.

Parvati adopted the son, and when Kartik was only seven days old, he killed the demon Taraka, thus fulfilling his destiny and the prophecy of his birth.

The story of Ganesha derives at both an allegorical and mythical level, and then again at the level of social evolution. The Marxist philosopher and historian D. P.

Chattopadhyaya traces the growth of the elephant god Ganesha from the position of a minor figure in Shiva's demonological forces to the all-powerful god propitiated by the priestly Brahminical classes and the common people alike.

The myths attached to Ganesha describe his birth as resulting from various mishaps, usually due to Shiva's irascible nature and uncontrollable temper. The most prevalent of these holds that the goddess Parvati was bathing, and so she created Ganesha from the scurf of her body and breathed life into him. This figure was set up as a dwarpal, or gatekeeper, to protect her modesty while she took her ritual bath. Her husband, the omnipotent Lord Shiva, was intercepted by the gatekeeper Ganesha as he rushed to meet his wife. Ganesha was of course acting as he had been instructed to, but Shiva was angered by the insult and beheaded him. The divine couple had a furious marital fight, and Parvati was inconsolable. Shiva had to de-escalate hostilities, and so resuscitated Ganesha, who was however still headless. Shiva ordered his attendant devatas to travel north and bring back the head of the first animal they encountered. This happened to be an elephant, whose head and trunk was then transplanted onto Ganesha's decapitated body. As the elephant-headed god, he came to be called Gajanana. As the head of the ganas, Shiva's personal army of spirits, demons and genii, he came to be called Ganapati. The ganas represented the ghora or terrible aspect of Shiva, and they were the dark or malignant forces of his all-encompassing self. Ganapati's elevation from their ranks to that of a major independent god is a typical example of the flux and movement apparent in a living mythology.

Roberto Calasso in his brilliant book, *The Marriage of Cadmus and Harmony,* examines the persisting archetype of the goddess intercepted while bathing, which he observes, has been recounted with many variations over the centuries: whether it be Artemis spied upon by Acteon, Athena watched over by Tiresias, or Persephone under the all-seeing eyes of Zeus. The mythic mind is a universal one, and to see the goddess bathing is to witness a rite of renewal and self-perpetuation.

The altering perceptions to Lord Shiva and his associated cluster of gods and demons reflect the movement of social, cultural and theological ideas. Up to the fifth century BC it is probable that Ganesha was synonymous with Vighneshwara, the demon of obstruction, who had to be propitiated to remove all possible obstacles. By the contrary and even perverse backflows by which the meandering river of faith which is Hinduism flows, this propitiation graduated into an acceptance of Ganesha as Vighneshwara, the remover of obstacles while undertaking a new enterprise.

Although Shiva is a phallic god, his reluctance to procreate, and the combined and constant efforts of the gods, devatas and sages to persuade him to part with the precious seed of his life-force form a typical motif of a number of myths and legends. The curse of Parvati, resulting in the childlessness of all the gods and goddesses in the Hindu pantheon, was but another facet of Shiva withholding his seed for the mortal world. Parvati resents her barrenness, for she is Prakriti or nature incarnate, and the natural state of Prakriti is fecundity. Yet incarnate as Parvati, the shakti of Shiva, she is not separate from his self, just as Shiva himself can never be outside Shiva. The glorious god is self-luminous, eternal. His delight in himself is manifest in Devi, the goddess. In spite of Shiva's asceticism and Parvati's austerities, his godhead is always in a state of perpetual union with the great goddess. This is what W.B. Yeats referred to in his poem on Mount Meru, where, in his mystic vision, he referred to the 'self born mockers of man's enterprise'.

The other important and ever-present member of the divine family in Hindu iconography is Nandi, the sacred bull who is Shiva's vahana, his totemic steed. Like the serpents that gird his divine body, Nandi emphasizes Shiva's aspect as Pashupatinath. Also referred to as Vrishabha or Virsha, Nandi symbolically represents the fecundating energy of Kamadeva, the god of love, the amorous and eager messenger whom Shiva incinerated with an angry glance. Nandi is sometimes depicted as a bull with a human head. He is the embodiment of fertility, righteousness, and stability, the virtues of an agricultural society. His master Shiva is often referred to as Nandishwara, the Lord of Nandi.

Let us visualize Shiva, the supreme ascetic, wreathed with serpents, garlanded with skulls. The celestial river Ganga flows from the crescent moon, which glitters on his brow. Beside him is seated his feminine energy, Parvati, the great goddess incarnate. Their self-born offspring, the elephant-headed Ganesha and Kartik or Skanda, the celibate warrior, sit beside them. In the foreground is the bull, Nandi, unshakable in his devotions. The divine family is not yet complete; it extends to the ganas, the host of ghosts, ghouls and goblins, the bhootas, pisachas, pramathas and other demi-urges that surround this ever-auspicious nucleus. All these dark, troubled and troublesome forces are the various energy emanations of negativity and uncontrolled, unharnessed vitality that are present in every life situation.

Another important figure in Shiva's theogony is Kubera, the god of wealth. Kubera was the lord of the yakshas, the elusive forest spirits who reside in ancient trees and secluded lakes, and are guardians of hidden treasures. Kubera is depicted in popular iconography as having a pot belly, a squint and a pronounced limp. He is kind and generous, but his devotions to Lord Shiva are said to have led to his becoming jealous of Shiva's wife Parvati, for he insisted that his own love for Lord Shiva was even greater than hers. This audacity angered Parvati, and she ripped out his left eye, which she later restored. Kubera is still known as Pingalaksha, of the yellow eyes. He is the guardian deity of the world's treasures, and the strange contradiction of the very embodiment of wealth being subservient to the great ascetic is as meaningful as ever.

Shiva accepts all his devotees, divine or diabolical, without demur. It is said, 'he who is rejected by everyone will find refuge with Shiva'. An anthropological understanding would interpret this process as the appropriation of the accretions of previous cultural and social mores. As Shiva himself is the representation of a tribal mountain god, the entire pantheon of demonology that he brings with him into the Hindu pantheon is thus validated and incorporated into the mainstream. Hindu myth is gregarious in the extreme, and its polytheistic appetite for co-opting anything it encounters is the driving force responsible for its survival as the world's oldest living religion.

Swallowing the World Poison

The duality of Shiva, the ambiguity of his auspicious and inauspicious aspects as Ashtamurti, can be understood only in terms of transcendence. The legend of the churning of the ocean and the swallowing of the Kalakata poison demonstrates this strange and terrifying detachment in the face of good and evil. In mythic time, the gods and the asuras were engaged in a long, unrelenting battle for supremacy. The gods went to Brahma for his advice on how to end the impasse. Ultimately it was agreed that the opposing forces would cooperate rather than fight. The gods suggested to the demons that they jointly begin the task of churning the oceans for amrita, the nectar of immortality.

The world poison, which could be interpreted as an emblem of entropy and dissolution, made its appearance in the Krita yuga. The Krita yuga is the first of the four ages, the Krita, Dvapar, Treta and the present Kal yuga. These aeons or successively deteriorating ages correspond in some ways to the Greek concept of the gold, bronze and iron ages. It is ambiguous and open to interpretation as to whether the deadly venom appeared first when the opposing forces of the gods and the demons had begun to churn the ocean for amrita, or whether the serpent of eternity regurgitated it after the churning of the oceans, when the Sheshanaga serpent threw up the Halahala poison after being used as a churning rope. Shiva as Neelka tha, the divine swallower of the world-poison, is but another evocation of Shiva-Mahakala, who will consume the time-world at the dissolution of the yugas. This cosmic, mythic understanding of deep and fundamental aspects of the mystery of life must be constantly interpreted as such and not dismissed as the fertile fantasies of an over-imaginative people.

The gods and the demons cooperated in the churning of the ocean, with Shiva as the mediator. As usual the gods played foul at the end, and won through subterfuge. Vishnu promised an equal portion of the elixir of immortality to both sides, and then, disguised as the beauteous nymph Mohini, he diverted the precious ambrosia to the gods.

There are many versions of the myth of the churning of the oceans. In the Vishnu Purana, Lord Shiva appropriated the crescent moon as it emerged from the waters and placed it on his matted hair. The thin arc, described as the sixteenth segment of the crescent moon, is not a part of the flux of the waxing and waning, but is the constant essence of the radiant moon-body. The cool rays of the moon shine forth from Shiva's forehead, the chalice of the moon containing the Soma, the elixir of life. The devatas extracted many priceless treasures from the *samudra manthan*. Lord Indra received the celestial elephant Airavata, Vishnu took Shri Lakshmi from the ocean and made her his wife, and the wily

gods appr...
joy and pow...
dualities, drank...
obverse and ine...
immortality. As he o...
stained by the poison, t...
Parvati, alarmed that th...
overpower him, clenched h...
poison. So it came to be that th...
auspicious one, is known as Neelka...
throat. Popular iconographic depiction...
with the deep peacock-blue stains on his...
Shiva among all the gods and divinities was...
by selfishness and greed when confronted ...
manifest treasures of the great ocean-churning.

58

legendary battle
in which Shiva
much decepti
common m
and vanqu
and his s
ethical a
of the d
and g
grou
can
ab
b

The consequences of this imbalance were long a
far-reaching. The malefic planet Rahu manageᴅ
somehow to drink of the amrita, and although Vishnu
cut off his head in revenge, Rahu forever enjoyed the
boons and blessings derived from that surreptitious sip.

Perhaps, once, within mythic memory, there was a
very real geographic *samudra manthan* here, as the
Himalayas made their way up from the churning waters
of the ancient waterbodies.

When Jalandhara, the son of the ocean, heard of
the subterfuge by which his father was deprived of his
many treasures, he demanded redressal. This led to many

s between the celestials and the demons, was of course victorious, but only after on and use of force. In all these myths, the tif of Shiva's dual role as both protector sher is in constant play. It is his immanence hadow which tread the ambiguous moral, d psychic ground between the opposing forces evatas and the asuras. The lord of ghosts, ghouls bblins, the ash-smeared frequenter of cremation ds is the only reality in whom the world poison be contained, for his ever-auspicious nature can sorb all that is negative while still retaining the illiance and purity of his essential reality.

Popular Legends and
Scriptural Tales

Hinduism is not a monotheistic religion, it offers many contrary and contradictory interpretations of its myths and scriptures. This vibrant polytheism affords a pluralistic and multifaceted understanding of the transient external world, with a singular core of meaning attaching to the deeper levels of understanding. It is interesting to examine some of the popular legends and scriptural tales relating Shiva's actions and exploits in this context.

Shiva's army of ganas and pramathas, interpreted by the sociologically inclined as being of tribal and aboriginal origin, were closely allied in many ways with the Shamanistic traditions and the core of demonology that remained from the ancient Bon-po religion of the Himalayas. Whenever the great gods tied themselves into knots by their own deceptions and ploys, they sought refuge in Shiva who as Bhaktavatsalam, or refuge of his devotees, cannot refuse the sincere pleas of anyone who worships him. Besides the unending enmity with the demons, the various scriptural annals and dialogues all record a degree of conflict and tension between the gods themselves. Nilima Chitgopekar sees this interplay as an attempt to mobilize and illuminate the concept of 'otherness' in gods of different geographical or denominational origin, calling them 'symbols of cultural coalescence and the amalgamation of diverse origins'. It is interesting and instructive to study the myths

surrounding Shiva with this understanding. The primary
source of this sort of material is of course the Puranas
and Upanishads.

The multilayered and multivocal myths that
constitute the vast body of religious literature contain a
historical core with accretions of appropriate and
subversive interpretations to suit the social and theocratic
expediency of the moment. The evolving oral and textual
traditions of the Puranas began with the Prakrit tales,
narrated at religious gatherings, which were later
recorded and translated into Sanskrit. There are so very
many versions and interpretations of this material that
it is difficult to interpret them in isolation. The sheer
excessiveness, vitality and multitudinous nature of the
Hindu mythic imagination manifests itself at its most
prolific in the Puranas, with the Shiva Purana being the
vehicle for the cluster of myths relating to Shiva in his
many forms, and associated divinities like Sati-Parvati,
Ganesha, Skanda-Kartik and the ganas.

Let us examine some of the more famous Puranic
tales, beginning with the destruction of the city of
Tripura. This legend, which occurs in several versions,
carries a multiple weight of allegorical and metaphorical
values. The asura Taraka had three sons, Tarakaksha,
Vidyunmali and Kamalaksha. These three asuras were
heroic in their actions, restrained in their thoughts and
unsurpassed in their austerities. The heroic penances of

these three asuras ca...
before them and offer t... 64
had stood in summer amon...
icy waters, who had thus defie...
and denied themselves all mater...
for the realization of this boon, a...
gift of invulnerability, for personal in...
impregnable cities to contain their forc...

Brahma agreed to give them what the...
with a conditionality. They would, he n...
destroyed if and only when they come into a s...
of vision, whereupon a single arrow would kil...
all. The cities built by the three asuras became fam...
in all the worlds. Tarakaksha ruled over a golden cit...
Kamalaksha held sway over a silver one, and
Vidhyunmali reigned over a city made of copper. They
were just and righteous, yet they did not represent the
interest group defined by the celestials. The devatas and
other gods thereupon petitioned Brahma to withdraw
his favours from the three asuras. Brahma pleaded
helplessness, saying that he could not possibly backtrack
on the boons he had granted to his devotees. At his
suggestion, the gods then visited Shiva and requested
him to annihilate the all-powerful asuras. Since the
asuras also worshipped Lord Shiva, he declined to harm
them. Lord Vishnu, the third member of the trinity, was
however persuaded to work upon destroying the demon

he ways of the celestials are generally devious,
the help of Vishnu they conspired to subvert
ng virtue of these asuras. Knowing full well
ir invincibility stemmed from their devoted
p of Shiva, Vishnu resolved to divert them from
ue path and delude them into worshipping false
. For this purpose Vishnu created a delusive teacher
Mahamoha called Arhat, who at his behest preached
Jain dharma to misguide the asuras. Or so the
uranic literature claimed, in an inspired attempt to
ubvert the successful Jain reform movement. The
Vishnu-born Arhat wrote a Maya Shastra of sixteen
shlokas in the Apabramsha languages. The false prophet
preached a deceptive philosophy and an alternative
religion, only in order to withdraw the minds of the
asuras from the worship of Shiva, and so leave them
vulnerable to the strategies of the gods and devatas.

The subterfuge worked, and the shaven-haired
monks of the new faith waited for the advent of the
Kala Yuga to work their plans. Narada muni, the
mischievous Hermes-like figure whose ploys and
malicious plans are the pivot of many popular myths,
stirred up enthusiasm for the new and beguiling religion.
Vedic rites ceased to be performed in the cities of Tripura,
and Shiva no longer granted the asura rulers his all-
encompassing protection. The divine architect,
Vishwakarma, was commissioned by the gods to build

a chariot for Lord Shiva, of which Brahma was the charioteer. The gods held the bridle of this golden chariot, the right wheel of which was the sun and the left the moon. Shiva, in his incarnation as Pashupati, sat in this celestial chariot and faced the asuras, who had so far enjoyed his protection, and the thought of destroying them awoke his sorrow and compassion. The tears he shed turned into the holy fruits of the Rudraksha tree, which are worn as beads by Shiva's followers. As Shiva fixed the Pashupati arrow and drew the bow, the three cities were destroyed, and the wielder of the Pinakin bow, Shiva himself, came to be known as Tripurari or Tripuntkara.

This myth can be deconstructed at several levels. The cities of gold, silver and copper symbolize the material elements of life. Shiva's arrow refers in an esoteric sense to the central nervous system, the seat of the Kundalini or serpent power. As the three cities of the asuras, correctly aligned, could be brought under the control of Shiva's arrow, so the mind can be brought under control through a convergence of thought and action.

At another level, the myth illustrates the process of cultural accretion, cleverly defaming the newly-emergent Jain religion. The increasing popularity of Jainism which was beginning to challenge the Hindu faith was thus countered by mythology and propaganda. The Puranic texts have always been especially vulnerable to such successive interpolations and reinterpretations. The format of the Puranas lends itself to a compelling blend of religious and moral instruction and popular entertainment, and so these texts become the natural vehicles of canonization and decanonization, of assimilation and disassociation. The Puranas are garrulous and digressive, but as a whole they constitute an impressive body of directed social thought and illuminate the successive waves of interpretation and reinterpretation of Hindu myth.

The Erotic and Ascetic
Aspect of Shiva

The central contradiction of Shiva's nature, the conflict between the erotic nature of his iconography and the ascetic nature of his actions and philosophy, is summed up beautifully in this translation from a poem written sometime in 900 AD. The poet muses upon Shiva:

> If he is naked what need has he then of the bow?
> If he is armed with the bow then why the holy ashes?
> If smeared with ashes what needs he with a woman?
> Or if with her, then how can he hate love?

The popular worship of Shiva in his phallic aspects leads to the popular misconception that he is a priapic and erotic deity. Nothing could be further from the reality of strict religious interpretation. Shiva, the divine ascetic, is the enemy of desire, the subduer of lust, the conqueror of love. His body is smeared with ashes, for ashes connote the very antithesis of desire. Bhasma, or ashes, are in effect the essence of fire, of virility, of the life-force, and yet they also represent its negation. Ashes are used in rituals of expiation in many and varied cultures, from aboriginal Australian practices to Ash Wednesday and the Christian theological concept of penance. They are the opposite image of semen and the phallic life-force. Although Shiva is a phallic god, his essence and substance is ashes. The death-in-life and life-in-death metaphor, of his asceticism and the transcendence implicit in it is best illustrated in the story of Kamadeva, the god of love, and his encounter with Lord Shiva. There are many overlapping versions of the Kama myth in the Puranic texts. In most of them, the flower-bedecked arrows of the love god incites the illicit passion of Brahma and the subsequent wrathful incineration by an angered Shiva.

Like Rudra himself, Kama too was an archer, but both their targets and trajectories were at constant cross-purposes. One of the many legends about Shiva illustrates the polarities between the erotic and ascetic impulses with particular charm. One day Shiva, the great Mahayogi, seated in Mount Kailash, was rapt in meditation upon the absolute. It was in the depths of winter, when the Himalayan ranges shivered and shuddered with cold, and yet were still not as cold as the austerity of Lord Shiva's penances. The gods, anxious as ever for Shiva's intervention in some celestial squabble, had deputed Kamadeva, the god of love, to arouse Shiva from his meditation. Kamadeva approached Mount Kailash accompanied by the youthful personification of spring, Vasanta. As the two approached, the trees and bushes sprouted buds and flowers, and all the forces of nature conspired to arouse desire and procreation. Shiva opened his eyes and was surprised by the unseasonal spring. Kamadeva aimed his flower-bedecked arrow at the great ascetic, and desire welled within him as a consequence. Angered by the intrusion into his meditations, Shiva espied Kamadeva, the culprit responsible for the disturbance. Divine fire issued from his third eye, and Kamadeva was reduced to ashes. Kamadeva's consort Rati, the personification of sexual desire, begged Shiva's forgiveness and pleaded with him to revive her husband. Shiva granted her the wish, recreating Kamadeva in the desire located in the human mind, as well as in the organs of procreation in the human body. As the destroyer of Kamadeva, Shiva is known as Kamantakarti, the one who ends all desires.

After Shiva had reduced Kamadeva to ashes, the uncontrolled fire blazing from his third eye spread havoc over the world. Brahma somehow subdued it and took the flame, subsumed into the shape of a mare, to the ocean's shore. The ocean asked Brahma what he desired. Brahma requested the ocean to hold and contain the divine fire until the dissolution of the universe. This intense mythic image of the elemental and enduring nature of desire only emphasizes all the more the nature of Shiva's austerities in subverting it.

It is only a superficial paradox that the great ascetic Shiva is also the god of the phallus, of regeneration as well as death. Anybody acquainted with the multifaceted nature of the Puranic tales, with their corpus of contradictory visions and points of view, with their

startling and convergent insights and worldview, can
come to terms with these polarities of the ascetic and
erotic implicit in the totality of Shiva. What may sound
enigmatic or elusive to more rational minds is an evident
and apparent reality to the Hindu mythic imagination.
Other cultures often find it more difficult to understand
and accept these contradictions. The Abbe J.A. Dubois,
an ardent student of Hindu religion, recorded his
shocked reactions in the beginning of the nineteenth
century. Here is an example of his outraged response to
the naked ascetic Shiva. 'By one of those contradictions
which abound in Hindu books, side by side with the
punishments inflicted on a hermit for his inability to
conquer his sensual passions, we find, related with
expressions of enthusiasm and admiration, the feats of
debauchery ascribed to some of their munis (ascetic
sages), feats that lasted without interruption for
thousands of years, and, (burlesque idea!) it is to their
pious asceticism that they are said to owe their
unquenchable virility.' This outrage was valid for the
good Abbe, whose chaste monotheistic mind was quite
understandably shattered by this flagrant debauchery.

Although the opposing aspects of Shiva's nature are
only apparently contradictory facets of a core unity, yet
there is a marked difference of nuance and
interpretations on the basis of Vedic and Tantric
understanding. The Pashupata Shastras that elucidate

the Shaivite path to liberation from the noose (pasha) of worldly existence through the individual soul (pashu) and god (pati) are coloured by varying shades of Vedic and non-Vedic tradition. The Pashupata is described as being 'outside the three Vedas and ineligible to perform Vedic arts'. The heretic sects like the Vama, or left-handed and sinister school of tantrism, worshipped Shiva as the divine liberator. Like the Arhat of the Jains, the Vama-panthi or left-handed sects were accused by the forces of orthodoxy of being created deliberately for the delusion and destruction of the traditionalists. The complicated worldview of this Tantric aspect of Shiva worship is almost entirely inaccessible to conventional verbal and logical deconstruction, for its very basis lies in accessing and entering parallel realities and logic frameworks.

The externals of this school of religious thought are best understood in the concept of bhasma, of the divine ashes that are at the same time both essence and substance. The Shiva Purana describes different sorts of Bhasma. The sacred ash or Mahabhasma is of three types: srauta (Vedic), smarta (resulting from smriti rites) and laukika (prepared from ordinary fire). The ash applied on the forehead is known as the tripundra, and it atones a host of sins and ritual omissions. Often, in Tantric rites, the bhasma is collected from cremation grounds, to indicate the strength of death-in-life, as against the life-in-death which is the basis of the erotic principle.

It is not only in Hindu philosophy and mythology that Eros and Thanatos, the contrary gods of sexuality and death, tread in tandem together. This is one of the basic paradoxes of the human condition, and Shiva is perhaps the most stark and startling representation of this unity of life and death impulses. The language of paradox and apparent contradiction is always useful in making difficult mystic truths more accessible. The almost perverse behavioural patterns of sacramental Shiva worship follow this truth, for the negation of socially accepted ritual and behaviour enables entry into other alternative levels of reality and belief. The followers of Shiva take their cues from the great ascetic himself. They conduct themselves as Shiva did. In the Daruvana, seducing the wives of the sages, he is described thus: 'At some places he laughed boisterously and terribly. At some places he showed surprise and began to sing. At some places he began to dance, expressing amorous sentiment. At some places he began to sing again and again.'

According to the sutras, the Pashupatas and followers of Shiva are instructed to behave in ways whereby they actively seek the insults and censure of those around them, for it is a part of their esoteric discipline to earn the active contempt of the uninitiated populace. They can thus deviously pass on their bad karmas to their unsuspecting revilers. These are all standard proto-shamanistic and cultic ideologies, devices for achieving isolation and worldly detachment. These devices for subjugation of the troublesome ego help subdue the desire patterns that lead to the need for sexual and material gratifications. These stratagems for detachment do not deny the daily realities of life, they simply despise them. Yet, unlike many other streams of ascetic denial, the Tantric way accepts and even confronts material existence. The five mystic tenets of madira, matsya, mamsa, maithuna and mudra, or wine, fish, flesh, sexual activity and parched grain use the stimulus of intense experience as a catalyst for entering other mind-realities. It is in these schools of Tantric thought and ritual that the contrarieties of Shiva's ascetic and erotic impulses are most corporeally united and reconciled.

The Vedic or right-handed approach to the worship of Lord Shiva is quite different from the Tantric, left-handed or sinister aspect. Shiva as the god of the dark side, the haunter of the cremation grounds, is worshipped by Tantric rituals through practices which to the uninitiated may appear orgiastic, necrophilic and utterly shocking, but which in their essential and metaphysical beliefs are in consonance with the deepest Advaita philosophy. The Kapalika and allied sects, such as the

Agama, Aghora, Kalamukha and Virasaiva, all follow
the secretive Rahasya approaches which seek, at the very
outset, to alienate, dissuade and actively discourage those
they consider unsuitable for initiation from approaching
their esoteric philosophies and practices. Much that is
strange and puzzling in these Tantric cults reflects
determined dissemblence. At an absolute level of
understanding, societal sanction and taboos lose their
sanctity and relevance; only those actually capable of
asserting themselves simultaneously as individuals and
seekers of transcendental non-identity are privileged to
leave the social group with its framwork of ordinary
human aspirations and seek to tread the path of power.
These cults seek a synthesis of bodily and cerebral
experience to achieve a Shamanistic penetration of
alternative and co-existent levels of reality.

    The erotic–ascetic polarities are surprising only
when viewed through the matrix of Christian denial.
Pagan societies knew no such contradictions, and the
sublimation of sexuality was never a denial of the sexual
life, merely a moving on. Spontaneous and joyous tribal
myths and practices from all over India attached to the
theogony of Lord Shiva, as well as the variety and detail
of diverse interpolations never deny the spiritual and
mystical understanding that the divine figure of Shiva
represents.

Shiva in the Daruvana

The myth of Shiva in the Daruvana encompasses and makes clear all the contradictions between the erotic-ascetic impulses and Vedic–Tantric interpretations of Shiva and Shaivism. The antecedents of this story can be traced back to the mythic past.

The constellation Orion was viewed as the cosmic figure of Prajapati, the antelope. The movement of the vernal equinox from Orion (Prajapati) towards Aldebaran (Rohini) was interpreted as Rudra, the wild hunter, aiming at Prajapati, who symbolized the annual cycle. This correspondence of mythic truth with the movement of the constellations is a constant feature in the deconstruction of ancient legends.

Bhairava-Shiva cut off Brahma's fifth head, thus breaking the sense of absolute unity of the uncreate and transforming it into the manifest chaos of the create. The paradox in this is that the fullness of the uncreate can never be depleted for it seeps into and permeates all aspects of the created world, especially those which symbolize the Shiva-Bhairava-Rudra manifestations.

The head of Brahma fell and he died. The head stuck to Bhairava's hands, to his left palm specifically, and could not be made to leave it. To expiate the sin of patricide, a common enough occurrence in mythic consciousness, compounded in this case by the far more grave transgression of brahminicide, Shiva in his form as Mahadeva made his Bhairava-Shiva manifestation

take the Kapalika vow. He henceforth would do penance
for this murderous act by collecting alms with the skull
as his begging bowl, until his sin was expiated, when
Brahma's skeletal head would at last fall off from his
hand.

So, Shiva in his aspect as Mahadeva-Kala Bhairava
roamed the three worlds to do penance for the heinous
compounded sins of brahminicide and particide. With
the skull of Brahma as his alms bowl, he came to the
divine deodar forest, the Daruvana. The deodar tree is
the most sacred of all trees. The word 'deodar' can be
translated as 'the wood of the gods'. When Agni, the
sacrificial fire incarnate, relinquished its body, its bones
transmuted into the trunk of the deodar, which sustains
its foliage even through the chilly Himalayan winter.

The hermitage at the deodar forest had many
learned and powerful sages, but they were for the most
part ritualists, more involved in the process than in the
ultimate goal of self-realization and release from
bondage. The sages, although they were recluses, were
not sanyasins in the sense that they had not renounced
their wives and families. Lord Shiva approached their
hermitage to beg for alms. The force of his tapas or
meditations glowed from his auric body, and it was
difficult to understand whether he was extraordinarily
handsome or hideously ugly. The Puranic texts, which
describe his appearance, are rather explicit. 'His penis

and testicles were like red chalk, the tip ornamented
with black and white chalk.' The handsome young
ascetic, his naked body smeared with bhasma, exerted
a powerful attraction upon the womenfolk of the
hermitage. The wives and daughters of the mighty sages
rushed out to greet the naked mendicant, for their
intuitive selves had not been layered over by ritualism,
and they could recognize the divinity that shone forth
from Mahadeva-Kala-Bhairava, despite the forbidding
aspect of his matted locks, his erect penis, his ash-
besmeared body, the skull he held in his left (vama) hand.
It was clear that this was a presence accustomed to
penance and austerity, yet the life-force in his manifest
form drove these well-born wives and mothers to a
demented level of desire. The comparisons with the
Greek god Dionysius and a state of Dionysic frenzy are
not inaccurate. The well-born wives of the sages came
with offerings of fruits and flowers. When they
approached Mahadeva they shed all restraint, taking
hold of his hands, pleading for his attentions. They shed
away their inhibitions, their ornaments, their clothes,
and embraced the naked stranger with the skull in his
hands.

This multi-allegorical tale continues inevitably with
the entry of the outraged sages. Their years of solitude
and penance and the hard monastic life were all
repudiated by the inexplicable aberrations of their noble

wives. Confused, pained, bewildered and also very angry, the sages asked the naked stranger for his name and identity. Name and identity are meaningless for a created manifestation of the uncreate, so Shiva-Mahadeva-Kala-Bhairava was silent. The incarnate Shiva put the holy men to the test, but they failed, they could not understand or recognize his divinity. Unlike their wives and daughters, who recognized the essence of this apparition, they were deluded by the power of illusion, by Shiva's maya, and they could see only an intruder, an outrager of their women's modesty. Angered beyond measure, driven in fact by the same frenzy that overtook the women, but in another manifestation, they tore off the phallus from Shiva's body.

The supreme mendicant, the Bhiksatana, was unmoved both by the women's adoration and the sages' anger. His inner calm was complete, for he was replete in himself.

In another version of this tale, as found in the Vaman Purana, Shiva appears after Sati's death, wandering the earth in his grief. In both versions Lord Shiva allows the rishis to humiliate him, for it is the way of the Vama-panthis or the left-handed ones to carry the burden of other's rational scorn with equanimity and forbearance. In different versions of the tale, Shiva variously tears out his linga or phallus himself, or allows it to be dismembered and torn apart from his body by the infuriated sages.

The severance of the linga from the body can be interpreted as an image of the dissociation of the erotic impulse, of the libido and life-force, from the ascetic continuity of the unmanifest reality. This highly paradoxical construction is actually quite simple. It was yet another example of Mahamaya, of the stupefication and wrong perception that accompanies the maya of all illusory things. The women who saw Shiva as the immanent life-force could not look beyond and see him in his transcendental role as the antak, the ender of all desire, the killer of illusion.

As Shiva's linga fell to the earth, all things moving and unmoving were destroyed. Yet Shiva without the linga is never considered a castrated god; he is not any less complete for discarding the visible symbol of procreation. What Stella Kramrisch calls the 'anthropomorphic metaphor of his body' has to be understood both with and without the attributes and symbolism of the phallus.

In many versions, the sages at the hermitage in the Daruvana realized much after Mahadeva-Bhairava's departure that the visitation from the Kapalika had been a manifestation of the great god himself. Anusuya, the wife of the revered sage Atri, understood the omens and portents and enlightened them. The penitent sages sought

Brahma's advice, and on his instructions the worship of the linga became established. Once again, as one version of the story goes, Shiva-Mahadeva came to the deodar forest, accompanied by his consort Parvati. The nature of illusion being what it is, the sages, now conditioned by Anusuya's explanations and Brahma's instructions, were receptive to Shiva's arrival, although the great god was, as ever, smeared with ashes, his eyes reddened, a flaming firebrand held aloft in his arms. They sought his blessing, and asked how they might best worship him. Shiva instructed them to observe the Pashupata vow, to concentrate single-mindedly on his form and image. Although Shiva and his consort then departed, yet the sages could see nothing but the glory and splendour of their remembered forms. This is a subtle irony illustrating the entire play of the create and uncreate, manifest and unmanifest, conditional and unconditional, qualified and unqualified interpretations of the world. It is not easy to break through the veil of appearances and desire to the essential self. The divine madman, the ash-besmeared destroyer of the ego, of illusion and comfortable appearances, is not an easy or convenient god to worship. He offers the consolation of neither moral relativism nor absolutism. There is no code of conduct, no easy categorizing, no promise of heaven or hell, only the uncompromising view of man and his god as a naked beggar, besmeared with the ash that portends both his mortality and immortality, a grinning skull on the palm of his hand.

The ambiguity of interpretation of Shiva as a benevolent or terrifying deity, of his light and dark aspects, is perfectly demonstrated by the lineaments of this tale. The difference of perception between the strictly ritualistic sages, who could only critically interpret Shiva-Mahadeva-Bhairava's nakedness, his state of absolute being, with the more spontaneous acceptance by the women, who operated perhaps at a less rational and critical level of understanding, is amply clear. It is important to emphasize that the basic doctrine of the esoteric Kapalika code, mirrored in the secret (Rahasya) mystic practices of other similar cults, is that of divine madness, of a contrarian doctrine of both surrender and resistance. This religious thinking, if at all it may be called that, does not partake of an ethical, moral or qualified worldview. It is a doctrine of absolute bliss and terror, an experiential and existential understanding, the purpose of which is to foster detachment. The seeming contradictions and paradoxes in the erotic–ascetic conflict are to be understood in this context and framework of understanding.

There are many other interpretations and substantiations of this primary tale. They take their cues, as did the rishis and the womenfolk of the hermitage, from personal and subjective concerns and orientations.

In some versions Lord Shiva violated the wives of the sages, in other versions he spurned them and left them lovesick. In all, he shook them from the complacencies and deceptive certainties of their unviolated lives.

The Worship of Shiva

The Shivalinga, which Shiva discarded, voluntarily or involuntarily, in the Daruvana, came to be worshipped as the visible symbol of his being. The sanctum sanctorum of every Shiva temple contains a stone linga, placed with a symbolic container representing a yoni or bhaga (clitoris or uterus). The linga is worshipped as a swayambhu, a self-born stone. A linga is the object of the greatest sanctity; it can be made of any material, shaped by nature like the pebbles on the river Narmada found at spots like Omkareshewar, or of clay, metal or precious stone. The etymology of the Sanskrit word 'linga' is charged with complex meanings. Linga decodes literally not into the specificity of a phallus. It is a word which translates best as 'sign', indicating a distinguishing mark, a characteristic of gender or sex.

The pillar form of Shiva, the Sthanu, or dolmen-like post, was a common symbol of the godhead in many early religious systems. It transmuted itself into the seed-bearing phallus, the symbol of fertility with which Lord Shiva had such a paradoxical relationship. Shiva is the carrier of the seed, which he may at will release or restrain. With the severance of the Shivalinga, with its abstraction, as it were, into symbol and metaphor, the cycle which began with Rudra the hunter shooting his arrow at incestuous Prajapati, ended with the voluntary discarding of the sexual organ. As the linga fell to earth, it shone with the searing glory of the created world, burning everything in its path. In the dark night of the ul where the demonic exhalations and dark energies excreted themselves, the flaming pillar of light extended across the universe, breaking the barriers between the three worlds in its awful glory. It fertilized the waters and impregnated matter with spirit. As the yugas, the cosmic aeons, manifested and remanifested themselves, the phallic pillar lit up the cosmic night, causing Brahma and Vishnu, who were arguing their supremacy, to investigate its source. Brahma, incarnate as a wild gander flew as far through the worlds as he possibly could, but he was unable to trace its beginning or end. Vishnu plumbed the depths of the ocean for over a thousand years, but neither time nor space could define the unfathomable vision. Admitting defeat, they saw before them the ineffable glory of Lord Shiva incarnate as the linga. So it was that the Shivalinga, the visible manifestation of Shiva's sacred power, came to be established in the inner sanctums of temples, as the omphalos stone, the very embodiment of Sthanu, the divine aligner of the life-forces.

The linga is always vertical, pointing upward as the phallus of the divine ascetic, with the veerya or semen rising up in memory of the primordial linga. It is a vertical stone, self-born, self-existent and self-perpetuating. This enduring symbol of manifestation and dematerialization, of the life and death impulses present in human nature, venerates the very essence of Shiva. It is more potent and sacred than any projected anthropomorphic image.

The mystic and charged nature of this symbolic understanding is reiterated in the sacred literature of Hinduism. The original philological interpretation of the word linga indicates a sign, a mark of gender or other predicate qualities. In the subtle body, it denotes both the essences of such qualities and their manifest condition, potential and fulfilment, the seed as well as the inherent death wish. So it is that the pillar of Agni, the sacred fire, is also the sacred phallic repository of Shiva's semen.

The luminous beauty of Shiva made manifest is also referred to as the Divyalinga or the celestial pillar. As the source and origin of the universe, it is also called the root-pillar or mula sthambha. According to Stella Kramrisch, the transformation of the severed linga to fire, and then into light, is an analogy of the experiences of the yogi as his body reabsorbs the elements which constitute it and he obtains a body made of fire. 'The epiphany of Shiva from within the flames, the pillars of flame and light . . . are precipitations of yogic realizations.'

Somvar, or Monday in the Gregorian calendar, is the day traditionally sacred to Shiva. Every Monday,

devotees, both male and female, fast all day to propitiate
the ascetic god. Oblations of milk are poured upon the
Shivalinga in Shiva temples across the Hindu world, and
leaves offered to propitiate him. Three things are
considered essential to the ritual worship of Shiva. These
are the belva leaf, (*Aegle marmelos*), the rudraksha bead,
(*Eleaocarpus sphaericus*) and holy ash or bhasma. The
belva tree is said to have sprouted from the sweat of
Devi, after she made love to Shiva. The rudraksha, the
sacred bead from the tree, was born from Shiva's tears.
Rudraksha beads have a hierarchy mirroring the caste
system of the mundane world: the white ones are
Brahmins, the red Kshatriyas and the yellow Vaishyas,
while the black beads are the Shudras. Rudraksha beads
are also classified according to the natural facets in their
shapes. A single-faced rudraksha is Shiva himself. Two
faces signify Ishana, and four faces represent Brahma.
Five or eleven faces indicate the presence of Rudra, six
faces Kartik, nine faces Bhairava, ten faces the Lord
Vishnu. A rudraksha with fourteen facets bears the
highest mark of Shiva.

Bhasma has a unique place in the ritual worship of
Shiva, for it is the essence of fire, or Agni. It signifies the
beginning and end of human activity as does the supreme
ascetic whom it invokes and propitiates.

The festival most sacred to Shiva falls on the
fourteenth night of the new moon, during the dark half

of the lunar month of Phalguna, some time between
February and March. This is the night of
Mahashivaratri, or the great night of Shiva. The day of
Shivaratri is spent in prayers and fasting, as it is the
night when the powers of Shiva are unleashed upon the
world. The night of Mahashivaratri is a time when
spirits, ghouls and goblins walk the earth, when ganas
and pramathas and all the other attendant familiars
penetrate the veil between the worlds. Leaves of the belva
and mango tree are offered on Shivalingas. A coconut is
placed upon a brass vessel or pot and wrapped with a
single strip of cloth. The fibrous husk of the coconut is
symbolic of the matted hair of the divine ascetic, and
the three black spots on the body of the coconut
symbolize the three eyes of the great lord. The linga is
worshipped by bathing it with the five sacred gifts of
the cow, the panchagavya: milk, buttermilk, clarified
butter, cow urine and cow dung. The pancham, the five
immortal foods, are also thus offered, these being milk,
curd, clarified butter, honey and tulsi or basil leaf.

The month of Sawan is also sacred to Shiva,
especially on the Ekadashi or eleventh day of the lunar
calendar. During this time, groups of eleven or forty-
four priests chant the sacred hymns and mantras
invoking Rudra-Shiva. The eleven subsidiary Rudras,
born of Kamadhenu, the wish-fulfilling cow, are
symbolic of the eleven pranic energies. The larger

pantheon of thirty-three Vedic gods is also propitiated on Mahashivaratri. Of these eleven are Rudras, eight Vasus, twelve Adityas, eight Ashvins. The representations of the Rudras are diverse and all encompassing. The following is a description of the various Rudra forms.

Aja-Ekapad, Rudra as the one-footed goat, a symbol of infinity, represents the element of fire. **Ahir budhnya,** or **Ahi-Vrita,** is the element of water in the manifestation of the primeval sea-dragon. **Tvashtr** or **Bahurupa** is a Morpheus-like figure representing the process of continuity and change.

Virupaksha is the symbol of the subjectivity of vision, and translates literally as 'the eye that creates different forms'. **Raivata** is a Rudra sacred to Revati, the presiding constellation of the animal world and Pushan, symbolizing the nourishing life forces. **Hara,** in contrast to Raivata, is the depleter, the thief of life and time. **Tryambaka** is the three-eyed manifestation of Rudra, symbolizing the different metaphysical aspects of the number three. These include the three states of consciousness: waking, dreaming and dreamlessness; and the three divine mothers, Amba, Ambika and Ambalika, representing mind, life and matter. **Savitra** the shining Rudra, derives its nourishing strength from the sun. **Jayanta** or the Victorious One symbolizes the divine life-force as represented in Lord Indra, the centrifugal force that drives the world. **Aparajita** is the unvanquished one, the positive energy derivative of Lord Vishnu. Aparajita represents the centripetal forces of nature, and together, Jayanta and Aparajita sustain the rhythm of the universe. **Pinaki** is the wielder of the bow, one of the destructive aspects of Shiva. Shiva's bow, the mighty Pinaka, is the instrument of his mastery over time.

The Twelve Jyotirlingas

The different aspects of Shiva worship have manifested themselves in the form of countless temples all over the country, the holiest of which are considered the twelve jyotirlingas. In the jyotirlinga form, Shiva is worshipped as light or fire. A jyotirlinga is said to be of divine origin, and each one has a unique legend associated with its creation. These divine lingas are spread from Kedarnath in Uttaranchal in the extreme north, to the southernmost in Rameshwaram, Tamil Nadu.

Somnath in the Saurashtra region of Gujarat is one of the most important jyotirlingas. It is said that Soma, also known as Chandra, or the personified aspect of the moon, was married to the twenty-seven daughters of Daksha. Soma maintained one favourite, Rohini, causing the sisters to complain to their father. He cursed Soma with consumption, upon which the moon-god begged him for forgiveness. Daksha asked Rohini and Soma to perform penance in this area, which they did for four thousand years. At the end of their penance, Shiva was so impressed by their meditation that he himself appeared to bless them. He proclaimed that the moon would now wax for fifteen days of the month and wane for the other fifteen, and thereby not waste away completely. It was in gratitude for this that Soma installed the linga, thereafter known as Somnath because it was at this spot that Soma, or Chandra, regained his radiance.

The **Mallikarjuna** shrine lies by the Krishna river in Andhra Pradesh. According to legend, one of the kings of Chandraguptapura fell in love with his own daughter, upon which she cursed him and he drowned. After this, she gave up all her worldly ties and became an ascetic. She lived here amongst the cowherds, and one day, she noticed that one particular cow would always return without milk in her udders after grazing. After some investigation, she found that the cow would discharge her milk over a linga. That same night, Shiva came to her in a dream and told her that he was present in that very linga. She then built a temple over the linga and worshipped it by offering mallika or jasmine flowers, giving it the name Mallikarjuna. It is said that a devotee's truest desires are granted at this temple.

Mahakaleshwar, located on the banks of the river Ksipra in the holy city of Ujjain, is one of the main religious attractions in Madhya Pradesh. According to folklore, Lord Vishnu and Lord Shiva met here and actually worshipped each other, offering holy belva leaves in prayer. There is another story that describes an incident involving a Brahmin called Vedapriya, who lived in the nearby ashram of Krishna's guru, Sandipani. A rakshasa attempted to conquer the city, and the Brahmans were defenceless with no army to protect them. They prayed to Lord Shiva to protect them at this jyotirlinga. When the demon attacked, the earth parted under him and Shiva appeared in his terrible aspect of Mahakala, instantly reducing the army of demons and rakshasas to ashes. The jyotirlinga was since known as Mahakaleshwar.

Omkareshwar exists at the confluence of the rivers Narmada and Kaveri. It is an island one mile long and half a mile wide, shaped like the sacred syllable Om. The linga here is worshipped with thirty thousand earthen lamps made daily by twenty-two bhaktas. There is an interesting legend associated with this spot. Sage Narada mocked the Vindhya mountains by comparing them to the scared mountain Meru, saying they could never achieve the same level of divinity. The distressed Vindhya mountains pleaded to Lord Shiva to somehow help them, and he did this by constructing an earthen linga in Omkara. It is also said that one hundred yagnas were performed at this spot by the king of the solar dynasty, Mandhata.

Kedarnath, in the Tehri-Garwhal district of Uttaranchal, is one of the most revered pilgrimage spots in the country. It is said to have been visited by the Pandavas several times. After their victory over the Kauravas at Kurukshetra, the Pandavas attempted to atone for the sin of fratricide by worshipping Lord Shiva at Kashi. He remained elusive, and they persistent. Shiva left Kashi to test their devotion and appeared in

Kedarnath in the guise of a bull. Bhima recognized him, and tried to chase him, but Shiva dived into the earth and vanished, leaving only the hump of the bull, which is till today worshipped in the form of a linga. The other parts landed in different directions, the face falling at Rudranath, his belly at Madmaheshwar, his locks at Kalpeshwara and his arms at Tunganath. All these five shrines, the holiest of which is Kedarnath, are collectively known as Panch-Kedar. It is here that Parvati worshipped Lord Shiva to unite with him in the form of Ardhanarishwara. Another legend recounts how the two incarnations of Vishnu, Nar and Narayana, worshipped Shiva at Badrikashramam, and pleaded with Shiva to take up permanent abode at Kedarnath, in the form of a jyotirlinga. It is also said to be the spot where Adi Shankaracharya was last seen before he went into the forest, never to return.

Bhima Shankara is situated in the Sahyadri range in Bhavagiri, near Khed in Maharashtra. It is also the source of the river Bhima, which flows south-east and merges with the Krishna near Raichur. The legend goes that Shiva took abode here in the form of Bhima atop the Sahyadri hills, and the sweat that flowed from his body after the battle with the demon Tripurasura formed the Bhimarathi river.

Kashi Vishveshwara, also known as Benares, is said to be the oldest living city in the world and this is one of the most revered pilgrimage sites in India. The jyotirlinga at Kashi is in the form of a cosmic egg. It is here that Shiva is worshipped as the bestower of worldly pleasures and salvation, for, after their marriage, Parvati chose Kashi as their abode. She is revered here as Annapurna, the giver of food, because she herself never ate before each and every one of her devotees had eaten. It is said that a king called Divodasa ruled Kashi at that time, but was not keen to leave after Shiva chose it as his abode. Shiva created a consciousness in him that made him forget worldly matters, and he soon left Kashi on his own. Shiva himself is said to have installed the jyotirlinga at Kashi.

Triyambakeshwar is in Maharashtra, near the town of Nasik. The origins of the temple are associated with the legend of a rishi called Gautama. It is believed that he lived here with his wife Ahilya. There seem to be more than one version of how he was cursed with the sin of cow slaughter. One story says that Gautama gave shelter to some rishis and their families during a severe drought, but the wives of these rishis were resentful at having to wait for Gautama's disciples to draw water from the well before them. After the drought, the rishis were ready to leave, but Gautama asked them to stay on. Not wanting to annoy him, the rishis planned a distraction. They made Lord Ganesha appear in the form of a cow grazing near the ashram. When Gautama tried to chase it away, it died, and he had to atone for the sin of cow slaughter by praying for the river Ganga to appear, which she refused to do. At this, Lord Shiva himself hid his tresses at Triyambakeshwara and forced Ganga to flow here, giving it the name Godavari. Another version claims that Gautama had been given a boon by Varuna that his granary would always be full of food and grain, the proverbial cornucopia. The other rishis were jealous of his good fortune and sent a cow into his granary and caused it to die while Gautama tried to chase it away. It was then that Lord Shiva appeared to help him atone his sin with the help of the Ganga, and stayed on in the form of Triyambakeshwara. It is here that the Simhasta Parvani occurs once every twelve years, when the planet Jupiter enters the Leo constellation. It is considered a very auspicious time, when all the earth's sacred waters are thought to collect in the Kushavarta tirtha, which is a tank with steps on all four sides. This spot, where Gautama Rishi finally secured Ganga on earth is considered extremely holy.

Vaidyanath in the Beed district of Marathwada is the symbol of Vaidyanath, the celestial physician, and is associated with good health and longevity. It is here that the sage Markandeya was saved from death by Lord Shiva himself. This shrine is also associated with the legend of Ravana, a devout bhakta of Lord Shiva. Ravana meditated intensely on Shiva, praying that he

would come to Lanka, thus making his kingdom
invincible. In his enthusiasm, he tried to lift Mount
Kailasha and take it with him to Lanka. Shiva was
infuriated and crushed Ravana with just one finger.
Ravana pleaded and begged for mercy. Lord Shiva
relented and agreed to give him one of the jyotirlingas
to take back with him, but with the warning that if it
was put down anywhere along the way, it would not be
possible to move it again. When Ravana began his
journey back to his capital, Lord Varuna, the god of
water, entered him and he urgently needed to relieve
himself. At the same time, Vishnu appeared in the form
of a young boy and offered to hold the jyotirlinga while
Ravana did the needful. But as soon as Ravana left,
Vishnu immediately placed the jyotirlinga on the ground,
causing it to become rooted to the spot. Ravana was so
angry and disappointed that he cut off nine of his ten
heads as penance for his folly. Shiva then appeared in
the form of Vaidyanath, the divine physician, and
restored his heads, giving the jyotirlinga its name.

Naganath, as the name implies, is associated with
Lord Shiva as the lord of snakes. Shiva had granted one
boon to the asuras for their worship. But instead of
furthering their worship, they chose to terrorize and
harass the devatas. The demon Darukaa and his wife
Darukii were given an area called Darukaavana where
the devatas were forbidden from entering to save them

from being persecuted. Here the asuras started to worship Shiva, and their chanting of the mantra, Om Namah Shivay, was so resonant that it disturbed even Lord Shiva in Mount Kailasha, who descended to punish them. At that time, he was covered with snakes, or nagas. In this form he is known as Nageshwara. He killed Darukaa, who had been harassing his devotee Supriya, and continues to reside in the jyotirlinga in the form of the destroyer of evil. It is said that even Parvati lives in this jyotirlinga in the form of Nageshwari.

Rameshwaram is by the banks of the ocean in Tamil Nadu. It is named after Shri Rama, who was the seventh incarnation of Lord Vishnu. It is said that he was advised by some rishis to install a linga and worship it. He requested Hanuman to go to Mount Kailasha and bring one for him. But as the mahurat, or auspicious time to install the linga drew nearer, Hanuman had not yet returned. Instead, Rama asked Sita to make a linga out of earth, which he then installed at the right time. Just then, Hanuman returned and Rama asked him to remove the other linga and install the one he had brought. But he could not even budge the linga, as it had the collective power of both Rama and Sita. So Hanuman's linga was installed alongside the existing one, and came to be known as Hanumandeshvara. Another version says that Hanuman brought the linga known as Vishwanathan from Benares. This spot is also known as the Benares of the south, and is one of the holiest pilgrimage sites in south India. It is also the southernmost jyotirlinga in the country.

Ghrishneshwara, or Ghushmeshwara is an ancient shrine near Ellora in Maharashtra. There are a number of legends associated with this place, one of which is about a childless couple called Sudharma and Sudeha. Sudeha persuaded her husband to marry her sister so that she could bear them a child. Her sister, who was called Ghushma, performed the daily ritual of immersing a linga in a tank as part of her worship. She had a son, who grew up to be so handsome that Sudeha, overcome by jealousy, killed him and threw him into a lake. Ghushma was heartbroken, but continued her worship uninterrupted. Shiva himself appeared before the tank and offered to kill Sudeha. Ghushma did not want revenge, but instead asked Shiva to stay on there for all time to come. Shiva revived her son, and the linga was thereafter named Ghushmeshwara. Another legend ascribes the name Ghrishneshwara to the shrine. It is said that as part of her morning shringara, Parvati used to rub saffron (gharshana) in her left palm to make a bindi for her forehead. One day as she was doing this, a linga appeared and was known as Ghrishneshwara.

Schools of Shiva
Consciousness

Shiva consciousness and Shiva worship have evolved differently according to local orientations and cultural bias. The main streams of Shiva worship in India can be divided by geographical territory and philosophical interpretations. In geographical terms, we can examine the ancient and venerable Shaivite tradition in Kashmir, with its highly philosophical and esoteric treatises and traditions, the culturally distinct Lingayat practices, and the devotional cults of Shaiva-Siddhanta in south India. Shaivism and Shaivist practices also spread with the Indian cultural diaspora to South-East Asia, to Java, Bali, Indo-China and Cambodia.

The Kashmir school of Shaivite worship is monistic, and looks to Lord Shiva as the supreme and only reality. Also called Pratyabhijna, from the Sanskrit word meaning recognition, it takes a non-dualistic view of the universal.

In contrast, the Shaiva-Siddhanta school embraced a clear dualism. The body of Tamil hymns and devotional literature written by Tamil Shaivite saints from the fifth to the ninth century AD, known in their collective version as *Tirumurai*, form the philosophical core of this school.

The principal texts of the highly esoteric and cerebral Kashmir school are the Shiva sutras, written as epiphanies by Vasigupta. In this and other texts like the *Shiva Sutra Vimasini* (Reflections on the Aphorisms of

Shiva) of Kshemaraja, Abhinavgupta's *Paramarthasara* (the Essence of the Highest Truth) and numerous others, Shiva is seen as the sole cause and manifestation of the universe. Chitta, ananda, ichha, jnana, and kriya constitute the five tenets of consciousness, bliss, desire, knowledge and action. This unity of perception is part of high or ritualistic Brahminical Shaivism.

The Shaiva-Siddhanta school is famous for the enduring body of its hymns. These hymns, also known as Agamas, include poems like Sivacarya's '*Siva gyana siddhiyar*' (attainment of the knowledge of Shiva), Srikantha's commentary on the Vedanta sutras, and Appaya Dikshit's commentaries. The thirty-six tattvas or principles of this school are divided into five primary principles or pure tattvas which include Shiva tattva (the essence of Shiva), Shakti (the feminine power principle), Sadashiva (the eternal good), Ishvara (Lord), and Suddha-Vidya (true knowledge).

The Lingayat or Virasaiva branch of Shaivism takes inspiration from the Kannada vachanas or inspirational poems. Basava, or Basavanna, was the twelfth-century poet saint who led the Bhakti or devotional movement of surrender through intuitive knowing, in rejection of the rigid ritualistic Brahminical practices. Opposing the absolute authority of the Vedas, and taking a humanist and liberal view of society, the Lingayat saints produced some immensely moving poetry regarding the true nature of Shiva. Rejecting the sacred thread worn by orthodox upper-caste males, both men and women of the Lingayat community wear a small linga, a miniature phallic representation of Shiva, suspended from a cord around their neck, to indicate their devotion and religious affiliation.

All these schools of Shaivite thought are orthodox and traditional in varying degrees, but the world-order they uphold is quite different from that of the Vama-panthis or followers of the left path. These sinister Tantric cults follow the inner authority of the individual to achieve inner bliss and understanding. Tantra is an admixture of Shamanistic influences, the ancient Tibetan Bon-po religions and esoteric magical practices deriving from Vedic and post-Vedic texts. It seeks to understand and influence reality through the propitiation of a parallel spirit world. Some arcane aspects of Shiva worship actively invoke the Tantric forces through a body of ritual and practice, which may perplex and disturb the uninitiated.

The theological basis of Tantrism holds that the supreme reality has two main aspects: the male force personified as Shiva and the female energies as Shakti. These have to merge and find expression in the individual physical body of the Shiva devotee. The human body has a primordial residue of energy located in the Kundalini, the serpent energy coiled in the base of the spine. Through the practice of certain specific and secret physical, sexual and meditative practices, this Kundalini can rise through the Chakras, or psychic nerve centers until it unites at the Sanasra Chakra, described as a thousand-petalled lotus located in the human cranium. The ecstatic understanding of the oneness of the universe is the aim and object of these Tantric Shaivite devotees.

The Kanphata yogis, distinguished by the large earrings they wear, are followers of Baba Gorakhnath, the mystic initiator of a largely prevalent and active cult which takes an alternative view of reality from the prevalent hierarchical one. Kanphatas and other Tantrics seek understanding outside the deceptive safety of the social order. Like the Lord Shiva himself, they are 'outsiders', taking an intimate and absolute look into the nature of the world and conflicting and contradictory versions of reality, all leading to a transcendent and overriding personal attainment of the ultimate understanding. The Gorakhnathis or Nagpanthis incorporate elements of mysticism, magic, Hatha yoga and alchemy into an intensely personal creed that seeks Shiva understanding through an absolute and unflinching detachment. Like the Kapalika and Kalamukha cults, the Gorakhnathis draw inspiration from the original Pashupata cults. The Kapalikas, worshippers of Shiva in his manifestation as Kapalika, with the skull of Brahma as his begging bowl, and the

Kalamukhis, literally, black-faced ones, are both mahavratins, observers of the five great vows of the Tantric practices. In reversal of the Brahminical vows of celibacy, austerity and associated virtues, the Vama-panthis follow a contrary path of excess. Their creed of madira, matsya, mamsa, maithuna and mudra seeks to use the body and bodily pleasure to locate their Shiva identification. At an esoteric level madira or wine is to be understood as the element of fire. Matsya or fish symbolizes water, mamsa or meat is the element air. Maithuna or sexual intercourse has its esoteric equivalent in the element of air, while mudra or parched grain symbolizes earth.

The influence of the Hindu kingdoms spread east in the fifth and sixth centuries AD, both through the trade routes and the missionary voyages of Brahmin priests. The pre-existing veneration of the earth elements and the Shamanistic religious practices, particularly regarding the burial and worship of the dead, predisposed countries like Indonesia to readily accept the words of itinerant Brahmins and teachers. A large part of south-east Asia incorporated Shaivite practices and worship into their existing religious framework, along with Sanskrit edicts and the worship of the Shivalinga which stands testimony to the eastward spread of Shiva worship. The Javanese kingdoms too embraced an indigenous version of Tantric Shiva worship, with royal ascetics like King Kertanagara (1268-92) and King Angrok assuming the role of a Shiva incarnate.

Satyam Shivam Sundaram

Shiva embodies the principle of 'Satyam Shivam Sundaram', truth, transcendence and beauty. The art, sculpture and iconography associated with Shiva have a stark simplicity and sublimity that distinguish it from the more decorative styles associated with the rest of the Hindu pantheon.

The earliest surviving temple in the Angkor Vat complex in Cambodia, dated at approximately 880 AD has a central Shiva court dedicated to the sacred Shivalinga. Another contemporaneous Khmer temple, that of Baneai Srei, has a huge sandstone sculpture of Lord Shiva, with his consort Uma-Parvati beside him. The Dijeng plateau in the Java plateau, a high volcanic region with sulphur springs and lakes, was a region where the stark local landscape was sympathetically identified by local devotees with the awesome and terrible beauty of their chosen deity Shiva. Mount Meru, the centre of the Vedic universe and the mountain identified with Lord Shiva's abode (along with Mount Kailasha and Mount Mandara), also figure prominently as motifs in this cosmology.

Perhaps the most famous and revered temple complex associated with Shiva is the Chidambaram temple in Tamil Nadu in south-eastern India. The temple is dedicated to Shiva as Nataraja, the cosmic dancer, and contains early Chola bronzes, some of them dating as far back as the second century AD.

The image of Nataraja dancing within an arch of
flames, his left palm held aloft in the abhay mudra
indicating fearlessness, is one of the definitive and
abiding icons of Indian art, and one which has attained
an almost canonical status. This dance, the
Anandatandava or the dance of bliss, was first said to
have been performed in Chidambaram, where the spirit
and grace of Shiva are uniquely present.

Nataraja's consort in Chidambaram is Shiva
Kamasundari, which translates as 'the beauty of desire'.
She is the manifestation of his shakti, the active principle
of all that he embodies. The four-armed Shiva, framed
by a blazing aureole of fire, has one arm holding the
damaru or double-headed drum, symbolizing creation,
and the converse hand pointing to the raised foot, the
place of refuge from ignorance and delusion. Shiva's
left foot is raised in dance to bless his devotees. This is
the image of the mystic dancer that becomes a motif in
so much of the sacred poetry on the subject

A.K. Coomaraswamy, in his unparalleled essay on
this image of Shiva, written in 1912, referred to the
Nataraja representation as 'the clearest representation
in any religion of the activity of God'. The enigma of
Shiva, of the sublime ascetic contained in the
contradictory images of the wild and beautiful god, is
the essence of the beauty of these images. The
simultaneous fluidity and tension, the terror and

compassion, the taut aesthetics of these perfectly balanced paradoxes, are at the core of the representation of Shiva. Indeed, the formal sculptural principles embodied in this most central and enduring philosophical image are so complex and symbolic in every detail that it presents an integrated image of the unspeakable mysteries of the entirety of Hindu cosmology.

The massive stone sculptures of the cave temple of Ajanta and Ellora were conceived on a sweeping scale, determined by the huge and intimidating rock-islands on which they were carved. The central image at Elephanta is a magnificent example of mature and introspective sculptural traditions. Of immense size, and carved in deep relief, it depicts an elemental vision of Shiva in his cosmic aspect, with the three heads integrating three of the visible faces of Shiva. Stella Kramrisch, in her seminal book on Shiva, describes it movingly. She says that although it has only three faces, the Sadashiva image at Elephanta is a kind of 'panchamukha linga', emerging from the dark depth of the rock. The fourth face, behind the frontal face of Tatpurusa/Mahadeva, cannot be seen, as the sculpture is cut out of the rock at the southern limit of the temple cave. The image confronts the devotee with three of its heads rising from one broad bust and base. The fifth face, the one in transcendance, is beyond the sight of mortals and has not been carved.

The garbhagrahas or sanctum sanctorums of most Shiva temples disdain these anthropomorphic representations, and content themselves with the Shivalingas, the phallic representation of the supreme mystery. The humblest pebble or stone which is elevated to Shivahood through ritual worship assumes the beauty, grace and awe of the concept it represents, which is in any case intrinsic to its essential self—for in this world, all is Shiva.

It is important to remember that within the Hindu system of aesthetics, the visual, plastic and performing arts were always completely integrated in their sacred aspects. These representations of Shiva were not static stone or bronze images: they came alive to ritual dance, as to poetry and literature, which reflected the same aesthetics. The poets, artists, sculptors and dancers who devoted themselves to these representations of Shiva did so with total surrender, they consecrated themselves and in a way became Shiva.

Percussion, rhythm, an intense sense of communion were essential components of the mystery of Shiva. As the divine dancer, one of Shiva's symbols is the damaru or the double-headed drum. Much of eastern religion uses drums to create or imitate thunder, and percussion is often an aid to ecstatic spiritual communication. In that sense, drums are cult or ceremonial instruments, often associated with consecration and sacrifice, as Shiva the dancer invokes sound to awaken and arouse the inner self.

The literary traditions, both folk and classical, have also always delighted in Shiva lore. The high Sanskrit style of Kalidasa's mahakavya, the *Kumar sambhava*, an epic poem written in the third century BC, describes the meditations of Shiva being disturbed by the beauteous Parvati, and progresses in the course of eight cantos to their wedding and the births of Skanda-Kartik, the god of war. Some of the greatest and most enduring hymns to Shiva have been written by Adi Shankaracharya, considered to be an incarnation of the Lord Shiva himself. This sacred literature endures as the very backbone of the Hindu religious tradition. The moving and personal Bhakti poems of the Nayanar saints displayed another kind of genius, a less formal, more intense immersion in the concept and totality of the Lord Shiva. The lives of the great Shaivite saints were documented by them in epic style in the twelfth-century Periya puranam.

The vachanas of the Virsaiva saints performed a similar function of personalizing Shiva as a deity, and bringing an element of social reform to an over-rigid Brahminical hierarchy. Palkuruki Somanatha was a thirteenth-century Telugu Shaiva poet who wrote the Vrsadhipa Satakam, consisting of multi-lingual devotional verses in Tamil, Kannada, Marathi, Sanskrit and Telugu, providing a pan-Indian platform for the Bhakti movement.

The constant and creative rointerpretations of the Shiva legends through popular artistic activities has kept the great god alive in the hearts and minds of Indians. Shiva is everywhere in India, in kitsch calendar art, in film songs, in folk motifs, in living prayer and ritual. Roberto Calasso says, 'Mythical figures live many lives, die many deaths . . . in each of these lives and deaths all the others are present and we can hear their echo.' As we trace the eternal living reality of Shiva in its forward and backward moments, in its multifarious and often conflicting interpretations, we breathe new life into the living faith of Shiva, he who is beyond words and names, he who is beyond understanding, who can be glimpsed only in the total and terrible moment of absolute surrender and annihilation.

Songs of Shiva

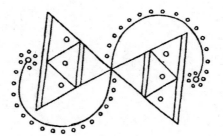

The rich
will make temples for Shiva,
What shall I,
a poor man,
do?
My legs are pillars,
the body the shrine,
the head a cupola
of gold,
Listen, O lord of the meeting rivers,
things standing shall fall,
but the moving ever shall stay.

                    Basavanna (from *Speaking of Siva*,
                         translated by A.K. Ramanujan)

I love the Handsome One:
he has no death
decay nor form
no place or side
no end nor birthmarks.
I love him O mother, List n

I love the Beautiful One
with no bond nor fear
no clan no land

no landmarks
for his beauty.

So my lord, white as jasmine, is my husband.

Take these husbands who die,
decay, and feed them
to your kitchen fires!

Mahadeviyakka (from *Speaking of Siva*,
translated by A.K. Ramanujan)